THEY SWAM

WITH THE FISH

THEY SWAM
WITH THE FISH

Six men from the Intel squad. Two are former Việt Cộng.

A Phoenix Advisor's Pictorial Memoir:
The Vietnam War and its Aftermath

CAPTAIN BOB LOEWER

RP

They Swam with the Fish
A Phoenix Advisor's Pictorial Memoir: The Viêt Nam War and its Aftermath
By Bob Loewer
BIO026000, POL036000, HIS027070, PSY022040
Print ISBN: 978-1-7366739-0-4
eBook ISBN: 978-1-7366739-1-1
Library of Congress Control Number: 2021903512
Printed in the United States of America

Edited by David Aretha

Remora Publishing
Venice, Florida
bobloewer.author@gmail.com

To the Vietnamese people who always looked at South and North Việt Nam as two reunitable parts of the same country.

Contents

*Two curious children in rural
Tân Trụ district, Long An
province, South Việt Nam*

The dense and dangerous nipa palm of the Mekong Delta

Acknowledgements

Thanks from an appreciative husband to Terrie, my wife and muse of fifty years, whose contribution and perseverance in facing life's journey with this combat veteran cannot be overstated. And equally, to my daughters Sarah Loewer Terio and Wendy Loewer Ciochon, two creative and determined women of whom Terrie and I are most proud, for their advice and sacrifice, particularly during their formative years.

I am indebted to the men of the Wednesday morning combat PTSD group at the Sarasota, Florida Vet Center. My lifeline for more than a decade, this group of men, in particular Thor Erickson, have helped many in its more than twenty-five-year history, including our combat brothers whose tour of duty has ended:

- David Sconyers, captain, USMC, two tours in Viêt Nam, combat company commander, college professor, dean of Arts and Sciences at South Florida State College, Fulbright scholar, Middle East expert, and a strong advocate of critical thinking. 1941-2020.
- Fred McLaughlin, Green Beret medic and platoon leader with MIKE Force Special Forces, and recipient of four Purple Hearts. Fred was a Vet Center counselor and team leader and worked closely with the Montagnard people of the Viêt Nam Highlands. 1947-2019.

The Vet Center counselors and staff members, many of whom are combat vets, have selflessly worked to ease the reintegration of former combatants into society, most notably Greg Cintron, Mel Yoshimura, Pam Meyers, and Fred McLaughlin.

A special deeply held regard and thanks to the cadre of clinicians who kept our mental engines tuned and have gone above and beyond the call of duty: Dr. Sabih Kayan, Dr. Maida Sierra, and Dr. Kelly Monette.

Finally, I would like to gratefully acknowledge those who helped me along this novice wordsmith's journey: Charles Wilhelm, author of *Wised Up*, for persistent encouragement to write this memoir, and Terrie Loewer, Ken Chapple, Jim McDaniel, Paul Hansen, Chuck Rieger, Craig Denbrook, Greg Cintron, Thor Erikson, Ed Bessery, and Jim Mackey for contributions and proofreading.

Foreword

With all its obvious drawbacks, the combat experience was not without some wide-scale benefits. Its military base gave structure and training to countless young adults, a sense of confidence in their abilities, and camaraderie unlike any they had known. However, while not all combatants develop post-traumatic stress disorder, for those who experience traumatic stress, the disabling symptoms make it exceedingly difficult to develop and nourish relationships. The markers of PTSD include anxiety, depression, emotional numbing, apathy, intrusive memories, survivor guilt, sleep disturbances, exaggerated startle reflex, short-term memory interference, poor concentration, anger at and distrust of God and society, hypervigilance, and the need to control but inability to complete projects.

Until recently, the prevailing attitude in our government was that not everyone should apply for Veterans Affairs services. That is, VA resources should be reserved for the neediest veterans. Unfortunately, this view not only fed into the combat survivor's guilt but discouraged qualified veterans from getting the support that would help them be better able to help themselves.

Why are some destroyed by wartime experiences, others broken but still fighting to survive, and some made stronger? Imbued by his parents with a love of knowledge, a deep curiosity, and a compassion for others, Bob has survived and is now sharing the story of his journey.

Terrie Klopfenstein Loewer
Venice, Florida

Preface

The Việt Nam Phụng Hoàng Program known to Americans as Phoenix was a counterinsurgency black ops effort designed and initially administered by America's Central Intelligence Agency. Within a year after its establishment, it was transitioned to a Vietnamese operation with aid and guidance from American combat advisors. Vietnamese Phoenix ground units, largely organized at the district level, were select military personnel who focused on the reduction and elimination of the Việt Cộng Infrastructure, the civilian political arm of the Central Office for South Việt Nam (COSVN). COSVN was the headquarters for North Việt Nam's covert government operating in South Việt Nam.

As I transferred to Việt Nam in July 1969, the US Army was rotating and replacing district Phoenix advisors, typically infantry captains, with Military Intelligence officers who often were second lieutenants on their first assignment. We were, as a group of officers, young and inexperienced.

The entrance to the primary artery through Tân Trụ district, called "Thunder Road"; it was frequently mined by the Việt Cộng.

In volunteering for Viêt Nam, I requested a MACV assignment, (Military Assistance Command, Vietnam) meaning a job as an advisor to the Vietnamese. I reasoned working and living with people of another nation was probably a once-in-a-lifetime experience and would enlighten, educate, and deliver experiences I would not soon forget. I was not wrong.

Advisors' duties could differ according to the assignment, but we were not US force officers with command time in the field. Nor, however, was our combat exposure limited to six months in the tour year, a common practice among US combat commands.

Vietnamese forces of Tân Trụ waiting for helicopters to land, extract, and re-insert them at the next suspected Việt Cộng location

As this memoir treks through my service in Viêt Nam and beyond, and my cultural enlightenment from the Vietnamese people, I remember the advisors of Team 86 with whom I served at the Tân Trụ district compound for their support and camaraderie. These men include SFC Charles Jones, the best mentor a green second lieutenant could ask for; SFC Mosley, always ready to teach; SP5 John Mullenax, our team medic and RTO; SSG McAlister; SP4 Mendez; SFC Crowe;

MAJ Ray Gravett, Infantry, the district senior advisor (DSA); CPT Robert Wooten, Infantry, the deputy DSA; and MAJ James Barnett, Special Forces and later DSA.

Each district in Viêt Nam had US Army Mobile Advisory Teams (MATs) whose members helped train and organize villagers to fight as militias against the Viêt Công. The principals in this effort in Tân Trụ district were all Infantry branch officers and NCOs: 1LT Nelson Brashears, 1LT Peter Heebner, 1LT Lawrence Blount, 1LT Robert Meyers, 1LT Michael Stefanchik, SFC Gardner, SFC DeYoung, SSG Johnson, among others.

As the Tân Trụ Phoenix advisor, I occasionally engaged in joint operations with an element of the US 2nd battalion, 60th infantry regiment, 3rd brigade, 9th infantry division: specifically, their Recon platoon. Prominent among them was 1LT Ron Pieper, 1LT Jeff Riek, SGT Ken Chapple, SGT Gibson, and SP4 Robert Mossgrove. Not all US soldiers were comfortable going into the field with friendly force Vietnamese. These men of the 1969-

Two young Vietnamese women wearing the traditional national costume of Ao Dai

1970 all-volunteer Recon platoon were among the most capable and integrated well with our hand-picked Vietnamese Intelligence squad.

Finally, I wish to salute the rural or riceroots people of Viêt Nam. Their cultural qualities were undiminished throughout the many years of war: respect for family, ancestors, elders, and the community. The personal characteristic of equanimity, the most prominent quality I admired in them, was there for all to see—forbearance under prolonged conditions of war. By the end of that historical period, the Vietnamese had sustained casualties of an estimated five million of their people, and another twelve million became refugees.

This memoir is a recounting of my experience in Viêt Nam as an intelligence advisor to the Vietnamese men who had never known peace in their lifetimes, and how that experience impacted the balance of my life. The story's chronicling comes fifty years after the fact, when I can remember the events without reliving them. It is the story behind the PTSD syndrome I developed, and a personal and sometimes brutal account of that which I observed and participated—it was *war*.

PART ONE

Getting to Know You

Chapter 1
An Ominous Beginning

By 00:30 near the village of Nhựt Ninh, we had set a defensive perimeter behind scant one-foot-high paddy dikes. We knew the dike walls probably couldn't stop even the smallest-caliber ammunition, but facing no other choice, we took up protective positions for the night. It was too dangerous to try a nighttime return to our compound through enemy-controlled territory. And we had no intention of getting back in the Tango riverine craft after the Việt Cộng ambushed us, bringing a dramatic halt to our planned raid to capture an important enemy shadow government official. Tonight, we had realized the first law of combat: *Whatever your plan, it will not go as intended*. We shifted from aggressor to survivor mode.

A Tân Trụ district rice paddy.

The six-tube artillery battery in Tân Trụ district, C/2-4, attached to the US 2/60 Battalion, or the 2/60 infantry itself would deliver parachute battlefield illumination until first light, nearly five hours away. The periodic night sky appearance of flares enormously aided in discouraging an enemy follow-up attack as we hunkered down in the open, feeling hot, sweaty, and vulnerable. Positioning ourselves to dodge the falling spent-metal illumination canisters was a guessing game, but we set that aside as a minor consideration now. It was not something we intended to complain about. The risk of being hit by a plunging canister, while potentially a lethal event, was an acceptable tradeoff.

We desperately needed the 500,000 candlepower bathing the perimeter. Forty-five seconds of light anew every few minutes might be enough to keep the enemy at bay and us alive. But at nearly five klicks out, we were technically just out of range of the illumination rounds from the four-deuce mortars. Operating in the sweltering tropical conditions of the Mekong Delta basin in a near pitch-black night, we could hardly call the situation worse.

The nascent crescent moon in the night sky caught my attention, and for a moment I finessed reality with the poetic sentiment of a well-remembered Joseph Conrad simile. *The young moon... was like a slender shaving thrown up from a bar of gold....* The thought of something sublime and so ill-suited for war forced a wry grin. This moon, even wrapped in the language of a master, could not help us tonight.

The illumination rounds were another story, although compromise was upon us again, diminishing their value. They exploded at their *max ord* (highest trajectory point), delivering barely adequate light, broadcasting from the west down over one side of our perimeter. We were directly at the foot of the artillery trajectory arc that peaked at about 600 feet altitude. We could hear the falling metal parachute flare projectiles spinning down on our position with a rhythmic *whoomp-whoomp-whoomp* sound.

We were still shaken from the blast trauma and shrapnel of the attack on our Tango boat that killed seven and wounded most of us an hour earlier. Through the eerie silence inside our impromptu perimeter so quickly pulled together to keep us alive until daybreak, we sat motionless, quietly waiting, listening intently for sounds of an approaching enemy.

As the hush was interrupted every few minutes by the *whoomping* pulsed fall of an illumination canister, the shock of what had happened gradually eased. My mind slipped away from this first week of Việt Nam service, back seemingly long past to a more secure time. The wisdom of the decision a year ago that was of paramount importance then had been made moot by a single 75 mm enemy projectile. That earlier time, a time of naiveté, a time of a pivotal life-altering judgment, was now abruptly revisited. The obvious question had pushed through front and center. *Why had I wanted Việt Nam so readily?*

A cadenced *whoomp-whoomp-whoomp* interrupted the introspective thinking, another canister impacting, too closely this time, from the recoil-shifted mortar. It provoked an instinctive jump, yanking me from the reverie. Reality was back. My head was in the rice paddy again, where I knew it belonged, in the middle of nowhere, facing a possible enemy follow-up attack at any moment. And here we were, with only the personal light weapons we carried, illumination affording us nearly a minute in five of eyes on enemy movement. But so far, so good. The perimeter was intact and defended as best we could. It was one o'clock in the morning. The question was, how determined was *Charlie* tonight?

An NCO from the American 2/60 Recon came over and reported there was no sign of enemy movement. Still, we were an easy target, isolated in hostile territory and without helicopter gunship support on station. He left our command huddle, heading back to his side of the perimeter. I thought about the adequacy of our defenses. Captain Smith, the infantry officer I was replacing, believed it was okay for the current situation. Smith was in an advisory role, too, but he had taken command of the operation after the wounding of the senior Vietnamese officer.

My mind turned to the broader tactical situation. I reflected on how this was my second op during my first week, coming under attack both times. It was as they had said. This was the Phoenix Program. But it begged another question. *Was this typical for Phoenix in Tân Trụ district?*

I would soon learn how it was to be and what I, as a non-combat arms officer in a combat slot, would bring to the table. But for the balance of this night's operation, we were fortunate. The Việt Cộng attack was hit-and-run. There were no further casualties from either enemy fire or the falling illumination canisters. Five hours after they triggered the ambush, first light appeared.

As we made our way back, on guard for an enemy encounter, my mind drifted yet again, trying to make sense of it all. This time, I recounted the events of this evening's costly foray, and thought about those killed and those seriously wounded. But despite the deaths of the Vietnamese soldiers, my attention was naturally drawn to my fellow Americans, the Recon men from the 2/60. I could not yet relate to the Vietnamese fighters, although their performance last evening was commendable.

It had been a long, tragic night. And for me as an inexperienced combatant, shocking. Over time, tonight would settle back into its proper context as I grasped the true nature of this war. I would come to understand the lengthy struggle of the Vietnamese people, the ones who lost seven men last night, the people whose plurality had but one allegiance. Not to the government in Sài Gòn (Saigon), not to the Việt Cộng or communism, but simply as riceroots people who dreamed their nationalism would someday lead to peace through reunification. And I would learn to set aside the cultural blinders of looking at this war only through American eyes.

Swim with the fish is the expression used by the Vietnamese to describe the tactic of the enemy avoiding capture by blending in with other peasant villagers. If I could do my job effectively, I could help my host soldiers target and eliminate the most dangerous in the Việt Cộng's shadow government, even as they swam in the friendly waters with the fish.

We arrived at our Tân Trụ district compound by mid-morning to somber but welcoming team members. There was an after-action report to be completed, and sleep to be had. And for the first time, there was an opportunity to confirm and treat my flesh wound and get cleaned up. But I had to drag myself through the process. I was bone tired.

As I peeled off the muddy jungle fatigues, I noticed multiple thumbnail-sized chunks of pulped human tissue and much larger blood stains from one or more of my fellow combatants. The flesh residue would wash off, but over time, the bloodstains on my fatigues would turn black and become a permanent reminder of the losses and horror of that evening.

But enough of that now, I paused. *Had I performed well?* My mind jumped back again to how far I had come from my training classes stateside, and the rigorous instruction I had received there. It was Officer Candidate School just eight months ago. We trained aggressively as a team for twenty-three weeks. I recalled the imagery of marching to class, a STRAC platoon of capable soon-to-be-officers singing a popular OCS song to the tune of "When Johnny Comes Marching Home Again." We proudly dared fate, sounding off the closing line of that song's refrain. *And we'll all be dead by the summer of next year.* Yeah, perhaps prophetic.

I was no longer convinced I was likely to survive this tour....

Chapter 2

A Fork in the Road

The underpinning of this adult life story was established twelve months before my assignment to Viêt Nam. It was no accident or twist of fate that I was in a war zone. It was like this....

The date was July 1968. I had completed army advanced individual training and was now a 71B20 clerk-typist, slotted to embassy duty in Bangkok, Thailand. It was a coveted MAAG assignment—a terrific position to be in many would say. But the entirety of my reason for enlisting was to become a helicopter pilot and fly in Viêt Nam. I was *gung ho*.

However, the edge of this naïve enthusiasm had been blunted by recent events. I was in the army now and had a better understanding of olive drab life. Decision time was here. The question was raised: Should a man with authority issues, a self-governing personality people implied, skip the posh embassy assignment, and follow through with Warrant Officer Flight Training, or opt instead for Officer Candidate School? "Bob", the recruiter advised, "as someone who wears glasses, you must put in for WOFT after you are already in the army. We can't do it as a condition of signing you up because that requires near-perfect uncorrected vision." And, yeah, I believed him.

Flying in the face of popular belief, my recruiter, SSG Moskowitz turned out to be true to his word. WOFT was still a choice. Deciding between the three opportunities was now pivotal. Waiting for the

MAAG assignment orders or putting in for WOFT meant a three-plus week, indeterminate wait at drab and dusty, hot-as-hell Fort Huachuca, Arizona. The base CO's standing order here was *If it does not move, paint it.*

I was a private E-2 trainee, subject to many extra duties while waiting for acceptance orders. And the delay was long enough that the clerk-typist assignment, the embassy duty in Bangkok, would soon evaporate. That outcome might well make me permanent party here, at the Arizona lizard trail outpost for the duration.

While I had no love for officers as I told him, my basic training drill sergeant, SFC Harrington, pulled me aside and suggested I consider OCS. I had scored a 140 on the Officer Qualification Inventory, the leadership test given to recruits. The qualifying score for OCS was 75. And a Fort Huachuca noncom, when I asked him what it was like being an officer, told me, *It is like sleeping on the floor your entire life and then having someone give you a bed.* Now it was decision time. The clerk was emphasizing I could be outta there forthwith if I applied for OCS. So, at the end of the day, maybe the decision was not so difficult at all.

One year later, an early morning insertion in the Mekong Delta. I was to be a passenger, not the pilot.

I set aside my piloting dream and elected to go to Engineer Officer Candidate School directly from Chairborne Ranger training, and after twenty-three weeks graduated with a class markedly reduced from the original number of over one hundred and twenty. Unexpectedly, I was given the opportunity just before graduation to forgo an engineer officer's combat arms commission in lieu of accepting a commission in the non-combat arms branch of military intelligence. The work of the Intelligence Community had always fascinated me, and I jumped at it. The engineer training of bridge building and blowing things up became a career bonus and would do well for me later.

To qualify for the MOS I wanted, Intelligence Research Officer (9666), I had to go *volindef*. A status of Voluntary Indefinite allowed the Army to keep me forever if they chose, perhaps not an unfair arrangement considering the expense they incurred training 9666s. After seventeen weeks of counterintelligence special agent school at Fort Holabird in Baltimore, I was assigned to a Military Intelligence group in Washington, DC.

The tasks at that facility included conducting background investigations for people whose job with the US government required an extremely high level of security clearance. While I was excited by the opportunity with a District of Columbia MI group, it quickly became clear it was a poor fit for me. The organization was rife with men whose career advancement seemed to be their priority, often manifesting as a staid, by-the-numbers, take-no-risks attitude. I left after three months by stepping up for a MACV assignment in Viêt Nam. Volunteering for duty in a war zone was *the* way to affect a nonprejudicial change of assignment.

In the words of the MI group commanding officer to me as I out-processed, "Being OCS, I did not think you'd stay long. This is a chicken-shit outfit." A stunner to be sure; such a level of candor is exceedingly rare in the Army, but I could not have agreed with him more. Regrettably, the CO was a man who admired action yet was chained to his bureaucratic organization, unable to direct the improvements he knew were needed.

And so, I was off on my way across the pond. One day and four flight hops later, I arrived in-country. The blast of stifling air as we deplaned signaled southeast Asia. And the thick wire mesh flashing over our bus transportation windows to prevent passersby from lobbing in grenades left no doubt we were in a war zone. Welcome to Viêt Nam, Lieutenant Loewer.

Chapter 3

The Scene Is Set

*T**hiếu úy mỹ*. Phonetically, tee-wee-me. That's *American second lieutenant* in Vietnamese. That is what they called me. My *nom de guerre*.

My enemy activity pin map, Tân Trụ District,
Long An Province, III Corps

I was selected to be the advisor to Advisory Team 86's Tân Trụ District Intelligence and Operations Coordinating Center (DIOCC). The Phoenix Program office in the government compound was about ten klicks east of Tân An, the provincial capital of Long An in southern III corps. The Tân Trụ compound was relatively small, housing five advisors and about twenty South Vietnamese soldiers, including the district chief, a Vietnamese major.

Tân Trụ was in the far northeastern section of the gateway to the Mekong Delta, an area of flood plains covered in sediment from the Mekong River. In the Delta, the monsoon rainy season runs roughly from April to September with June, July, and August being the rainiest months typically. The humid weather, the rains, and the near sea level terrain of rich alluvial soil supported the growth of over seventy-five percent of Việt Nam's rice food supply. The dense vegetation of nipa palm and mangrove was lush and deceptively benign in appearance. However, it gave the enemy forces shelter everywhere. Fighting conditions including perpetual high humidity and seasonal monsoon rains could be abysmal. That was not counting the ongoing risk from poisonous krait and cobra snakes, malaria, leeches, trench foot, and large bees that were known throughout the countryside for their lethality.

As I began my tour of duty, Tân Trụ and its populace were predominately controlled at night by the Việt Cộng military units and supported by reduced strength K4, K5, and K6 North

Vietnamese Army battalions from the first NVA Regiment. Operations reports from the 3rd Brigade, 9th Infantry Division in Tan An City in November 1969 put their combined strengths at about 660 enemy. The province name, Long An, meaning *peaceful dragon*, belied its security condition. During the period preceding 1968, the enemy widely controlled Long An province. Many North Vietnamese Army regiments and Việt Cộng battalions operated there, enjoying highly effective supply lines from the Cambodian Parrot's Beak depots, along the Vàm Cỏ Tây and Vàm Cỏ Đông rivers. Next to these waterways, abandoned plantations offered undisturbed concealment from allied forces.

By introducing the US 3rd Brigade, 9th Infantry Division in 1967, the control and freedom of movement enjoyed by the enemy in Long An ebbed. Battalion-sized operations resulted in major losses for both the NVA and the Việt Cộng, and drove them to employ more stealthy, nighttime tactics. Thus, while the benefits of larger force operations shifted control of some areas in Long An, it did not wrest day and night control of Tân Trụ district away from the enemy. The Việt Cộng operated less in the open and executed on more careful targeting. By the time I arrived in mid-1969, enemy attacks occurred sporadically from smaller, well-dispersed groups, but often were no less effective than before. While the years 1967 and 1968 are considered by the US Army a turning point in favor of allied forces in the war, in Long An the enemy influence over the hamlet and village riceroots people remained strong.

The dirt Road 225 leading into our district earned the nickname "Thunder Road" because it was an occasional target of Việt Cộng mine-planting sappers. They blew up a lengthy Bailey bridge on the road in September 1969, one month after I arrived. The Tân Trụ district compound where I would stay was occasionally the target of rocket and mortar fire. My soon-to-be new home came under

107 mm rocket attack three weeks before I came in, killing one and wounding three Vietnamese soldiers. The enemy had killed both US and Vietnamese personnel in the compound when it had come under fire. We had sporadic sapper probes in the perimeter wire and sometimes US snipers setting up for business in our tower with starlight scopes mounted on their precision M14 rifles.

Just across the dirt road at the entrance to our compound was a two-tube Vietnamese field artillery battery of about ten men. Sappers overran it, a grisly scene, six months into my tour. Nearly two klicks west of our compound, a much larger and more formidable facility housed the US 2/60 Battalion. Camp Scott, as it was known, came under an enemy ground attack seven months before my tour began.

We conducted military operations at all hours, during the day with a multi-squad or greater sized force. During the night when the enemy had control, the countryside was a free-fire zone. Ambushes were set up for select targets. Our Phoenix Vietnamese Intelligence squad held joint operations, going into the field with elements of the 2/60 Recon platoon.

Certain of our supply routes, such as Thunder Road, were under daylight control of the government of South Việt Nam. The Việt Cộng would occasionally interdict civilian and friendly force movement on that thoroughfare by blowing up its bridges and planting mines in stacked clumps of mud. Out-and-out firefights with people using the road were uncommon during my tour, but at night the Việt Cộng controlled the countryside, including the roads.

Tân Trụ had landmarks known beyond its borders. The Elbow, partially pictured here, was a staging area for the Việt Cộng during the 1968 Tet offensive, its bomb crater-pocked appearance suggesting past major battles; the Testicles, or colloquially the Nuts, the sites of Việt Cộng strongholds; the Bowling Alley, a vast flood plain under enemy control; and the Thumb, part of the neighboring district of Cần Đước east of Tân Trụ but somewhat like the Testicles, a geographic feature readily identifiable from the air, useful as a staging point for tactical aircraft.

Broadly, the district level Phoenix advisor's job in III Corps was to aid the continued successful implementation and operation of Phoenix, run by the Vietnamese military. When I arrived, Phoenix had been in practice operational about one year. Although initially established by the Central Intelligence Agency under the code name ICEX in 1967, they gradually transferred it to Vietnamese control. The founding "Infrastructure Intelligence Coordination and Exploitation (ICEX)" document, MACV Directive 381-41, was distributed on July 9 of that year. It charged elements with "coordinating and focusing the intelligence and operational attack on infrastructure, and with stimulating, energizing, guiding and collaborating with the corresponding Vietnamese organizations and effort."

A portion of Tân Trụ's Elbow. The Vàm Cỏ Đông
river is visible in the lower left corner.

Advisors were not seen as combatants, and strictly speaking, we were not. Indeed, Phoenix advisors were told they had no requirement to go into the field. But I saw no other way to quickly win the confidence of the Vietnamese men I worked with every day than to go on operations with them. Further, I had volunteered for Viêt Nam and intended that I get a full measure of exposure to that war. And unmarried and at age twenty-one, I was okay with that risk.

We used call signs for identification in radio communications. The call signs and radio frequencies changed monthly for security purposes. For example, the Tân Trụ district advisory team might be designated Happy Tanker seven-three. If a communication was directed only at me as the intelligence officer, a "two" was appended per military convention as in Happy Tanker seven-three-two.

Lieutenant Loewer, with some members of the Intel Squad immediately following an operation.

The business of Phoenix was to a large extent intelligence collection, analysis, and putting that information to work by ambushing the enemy. We were a reaction force that specifically targeted certain Việt Cộng officials in their covert government role. We often knew them by name and tried to intercept them in the field. Most operations, however, were unsuccessful because predicting precisely when and where the enemy would be was difficult. Often the intelligence, nearly impossible to gain in a Việt Cộng sympathetic area, was inadequate or faulty. Nonetheless, Phoenix

was a distinctly successful program, as noted after
the war by the commander and master strategist
North Vietnamese General Giáp.

My activities as the Tân Trụ Phoenix officer
included nighttime helicopter search-and-destroy
(called *firefly*) missions, night ambushes, daytime
operations, visual reconnaissance by helicopter,
coordinating chopper gunship support, and less

*Unofficial
Phoenix patch*

exciting but socially rewarding rural development tasks such as
helping set up a local school with a homemade blackboard. At
other times, I briefed many senior people because Phoenix was
controversial, even among our military. I presented to or helped brief
the syndicated columnist Joseph Alsop, Sr., Ambassador Bob Komer,
multiple generals including LTG Davison, and others.

I reviewed a lot of intelligence reports and passed on or initiated
operations to act on them. When in the field I contributed communications support; I called for medevacs and directed gunships when
needed. But, as my combat experience matured, I sometimes took

a more direct role in combat operations, a
move counter to my job description and
actively discouraged by higher command.

From my first days in combat when
it was all about trying to "will" my body
below ground level as we came under fire,
to my seasoned days when a senior advisor
NCO would ask to op with me and a province operations advisor, Major Ted Gesulga,
called me Little Tiger, I was satisfied with
my tour in Việt Nam. I returned after a year
in the field with both physical and mental
impacts, not uncommon to some who saw

*Major Ted Gesulga, Long
An province operations
advisor in Tan An city.*

occasional action. Most importantly, I gained the perspective of another of our planet's people, particularly the peasants of this beautiful country, halfway around the world living a dramatically different culture. Education at its finest.

But would I do it again, as is sometimes asked? Notwithstanding what the people of Việt Nam taught me, if I had understood the legacy costs of a year of combat operations in Việt Nam's Upper Delta, possibly not.

Chapter 4

Getting Down to Phoenix Business

As I arrived at III Corps Phoenix headquarters to start my tour in early August 1969, another lieutenant had come in for assignment at the same time. Giving a favorable impression to the executive officer, Second Lieutenant Cawood was assigned to a largely pacified area of Việt Nam, relatively free of Việt Cộng. The XO then pivoted and posted me to the Việt Cộng-controlled Tân Trụ district in Long An province. The stated reason? "You are OCS, Loewer. So, I am sending you to Tân Trụ. Cawood is ROTC. He draws the pacified district." I came to understand "pacified district" in this case meant advisor estuarial water skiing. But Tân Trụ was my destination. As Joseph Alsop Sr., the nationally syndicated

Lodging at III Corps HQs

21

columnist reported the following year, "Tân Trụ was a Việt Cộng fortress-district."

August 8, 1969, Day 1

After a week in transit and at higher headquarters…arrival! Tân Trụ district, reportedly home of the NVA regiment rumored to have shot down and killed a US two-star general. And home of eight-foot-long cobras, malaria, and aggressive bees the size of a half-dollar who knew they were a daunting fighting force, too.

I was the relief officer for an American infantry captain whose tour was wrapping up. As the Phoenix Program matured, infantry officers were being changed out, replaced with intelligence officers; that is where I came in. They designed the Phoenix Program to identify and dismantle the Việt Cộng Infrastructure (Việt Cộng civilian government) through various methods including infiltration, capture, interrogation, killing, and counterterrorism.

Advisory teams were often composed of a small number of army officers and enlisted men. Our group was headed by infantry major Ray Gravett, a tall, focused officer who projected an agreeable mix of instinctive leadership and ease with team informalities, important in advisory role dynamics. It was an air of quiet authority that I appreciated and naturally adopted, becoming the cornerstone of my supervisory style in later executive and technical careers. Captain Ray Smith, the infantry officer I was replacing, was still settling into his recent promotion from first lieutenant. Like Gravett, he was a capable officer who knew his job well. SFC Charles Jones and SFC Mosley were open, friendly men, eager to help this young lieutenant learn the ropes. SP5 Umlauf and SP5 Rosario were the team's RTOs who primarily worked our operations desk 24/7 although they, like all team members, got combat time in the field. SP5 Mullenax held two jobs as the team medic and occasional tactical RTO.

August 11, 1969, Day 4

The Vietnamese program, known as Chiêu Hồi (*Open Arms*), encouraged the enemy to rally to the side of the Vietnamese government. In offering this opportunity, they expressed the expectation for both sides to forgive transgressions and join, or at least tolerate, living among people of the other side. In the process, the Republic of Vietnam (RVN) government could gain valuable intelligence. But this was an aspiration that was generally considered to be of high hope, despite the intent of the national Open Arms program. First contact with our forces by a rallier—a Hồi Chánh—was usually when they surrendered by walking into the district compound.

My first walk-in under the Chiêu Hồi program to accept Việt Cộng defectors occurred this mid-Monday morning and was the most memorable. He was Lẽ Ching Hương, a Việt Cộng sapper platoon leader who had been operating in Tân Trụ for the past three months. Hương was talkative, although initially in a somewhat reserved manner. He discussed plans for the Việt Cộng and the North Vietnamese Army regulars assigned to Tân Trụ to attack both our compound and that of the US 2/60 Infantry division. But perhaps because he rallied to our side, the enemy reduced their immediate attack plans to firing mortars on our positions. That evening, the artillery rounds fell short of their targets and onto a nearby village, killing one and wounding four innocent civilians.

As we talked through my interpreter, Hương and I became more comfortable with each other. He related his story: At age ten, his father—whom he had not seen since—took him to North Việt Nam for school. Upon graduation from high school, he attended the air force academy in Russia where he was instructed in piloting the Soviet MIG-19 jet aircraft. Interestingly, among his classmates were two Cubans, a Czech, some Chinese, and Russians.

He became a member of the Communist Party. Apparently, higher-ups in Hà Nội (Hanoi), North Việt Nam, recalled his class one year before graduation in 1964 due to an exacerbated disagreement over the Nikita Khrushchev table-pounding incident in 1960 at the UN. At least, that was the reason given by the North Vietnamese to the Soviets according to Hương.

He enrolled at Hà Nội University of Science and Technology in late 1964 majoring in mechanical engineering. While a sophomore, he asked for a leave of absence to visit his mother, brothers, and sisters who lived in South Việt Nam. Angry that his superiors refused the request, he deserted and headed south in search of them.

When Hương reached his hometown in Long An province, he could not locate his family or any of its members. His only viable option at the time was to join the local Việt Cộng unit. Because of his Communist Party membership and higher education, he was made a platoon leader, a position he occupied until he rallied to the GVN (Government of South Việt Nam) side.

Hương remarked that he eventually located his family and wanted to openly rejoin them, his reason for surrendering. It was also clear

The extremely dense mangrove biome and its well-known nipa palm (nypa frutican) often referred to as "nipa".

he was unhappy with many things: the guerrilla lifestyle, the heavy-handed control exercised by Việt Cộng political officers even though he was a party member, and the prospect of participating in the planned attack against US and Vietnamese forces. He wanted to return to the higher standard of living he'd enjoyed with his family instead of continuing to live among the nipa palm, an extremely dense palm native to estuarine habitats, with his fellow Việt Cộng sappers.

As Hương was getting ready to travel to the Vietnamese higher headquarters, I said goodbye to him in Russian—about all I remembered from the one-semester college language course. He surprised me with "Das vedanya" (until we meet again) and shook my hand. Wow! Four days at my assignment and I had had a sit-down with a member of the Communist Party.

August 13, 1969, Day 6

It was time for my first op—a nighttime ambush we would set up hoping to catch members of the Việt Cộng Infrastructure in the middle of their night duties such as tax collection. We ventured out with about two dozen men consisting of the Vietnamese Intel squad and two squads from the US Recon platoon. As we started walking east from the Tân Trụ district compound at 21:00 hours, we weren't too far down the road when SGT Ken Chapple, in charge tonight of the 2/60 Recon men with whom we occasionally op'ed, asked me if I was a second lieutenant or first. I answered, "a Second." When he said nothing in reply, I asked if that fact bothered him. "No, sir" was his response. "Well, it bothers me," I mentioned. And it did—no combat experience, a non-combat arms officer, no Việt Nam training to speak of, and now going on a nighttime ambush as my first op where my job tonight was to observe and learn. His question was well founded—we had to know how much we could depend on each other. What was our level of experience and tactical expertise?

About four klicks into the field, Ken was second in line, making his way across a twenty-foot-wide river. The water chest deep, we came under concentrated, precise automatic weapons fire from about six Việt Cộng close in and directly ahead. All hell broke loose and being further back in line, not yet in the water, I dropped to the rice paddy mud. I hoped sheer willpower would force my body to move below the surface of this relatively flat terrain. After a few seconds of *I am in the war now, Mom* kind of thinking, I rolled toward my left to reach my right jungle fatigue cargo pants pocket. I grasped and quickly passed around the half-dozen handheld parachute flares CPT Smith had asked me to carry.

First Lieutenant
Bob Loewer

Meanwhile, Ken was taking a hail of bullets hitting in the water next to him, some splattering river water on his face and body that felt like blasted sand. Our red tracer bullets and the enemy green

The **M127A1 white star parachute signal flares** were launched by removing the top cap, placing it on the bottom of the flare, and striking the cap upward toward the sky with the heel of the hand. The rocket fuel was ignited, starting the motor, and sending the fin-guided flare up to about eight hundred feet altitude. They were remarkable; they brought 125,000 candlepower lighting up the battlefield for nearly half a minute while descending slowly to the ground. They were highly portable at ten inches in length in an aluminum tube weighing about a pound.

tracers abounded. The Vietnamese among us popped the flares almost simultaneously. It lit up the area as if it were a bright daylight that slowly turned to yellow as the flare magnesium burned away. The Intel and Recon squads returned fire. Ken quickly ordered his men to pull back, not being able to escape their vulnerable position in the water fast enough.

The small Việt Cộng group broke contact, and it was over nearly as quickly as it began without a clear casualty on either side. None of us were wounded, and no enemy blood trails were visible. It surprised Ken neither he nor the Recon point man were casualties. It was a Việt Cộng ambush tactic to shoot intensely, then quickly withdraw and merge with the local people before American resources such as artillery or gunships could be brought to bear. It was *swimming with the fish*, a highly effective ploy, one the famous enemy general, Võ Nguyên Giáp, well understood.

We would later learn that the contact was not incidental. The enemy knew we were coming, and we had tripped *their* ambush. An experienced combatant admonished me for giving out the flares too quickly. I am not sure I agreed with that assessment, but to be fair, the handheld illumination flares were incredibly useful and difficult to obtain. It is not clear whether the near-blinding light from the sudden flare popping endangered the men caught gear-laden and chest deep midway crossing the river, or revealed the enemy position enough forcing them to break contact and withdraw.

Major Ray Gravett, district senior advisor

Returning to our compound, infantry Captain Ray Smith briefed Major Gravett on the operation. Ray Gravett's comment, inspecting his mud-soaked new Phoenix officer returned from his first op, was, "Outstanding!" It was boot-camp, Việt Nam style.

August 14, 1969, Day 7

At this moment back in the World, twelve time zones away, a major counterculture event was being birthed under the name Woodstock. Attracting over 400,000 of our peers, it was a touchstone occasion for many of us both at home and at war, exemplifying the spirit of the Woodstock generation. Our business this evening, however, was not with Jimi Hendrix, CCR, Janis, the Who, or the Dead. Although sadly, as we would learn, there would be dead involved soon enough.

We headed back to the same target, this time in greater Vietnamese force and with more US 2/60 Recon members. We boarded two modified LCM boats (Army Armored Troop Carriers called Tangos) likely from the US Navy Task Force 117. They were stationed in Tân An at the Navy Boat Yard and traveled eastward along the Vàm Cỏ Tây river toward our destination. The modified Tangos, seventeen meters long and displacing sixty-six tons, were designed to be both a troop carrier and assault craft. They were heavily armored with high-hardness XAR-30-type steel and bar armor. The Tango's armor against .50-caliber machine guns and antitank rounds up to 57 mm provided some ballistic protection for the crew and passengers. But they could not withstand, as the enemy well-understood, the shape charge explosive housed in a 75 mm armor-piercing round.

Earlier in the evening, on their way to pick us up at the embarkation point, the Tango boats were fired upon by an unknown sized enemy force with small arms fire. SGT Chapple informed the Echo Company master sergeant of the attack and checked to determine if the operation was still something in which Recon would take part.

The MSG scolded, "What do you think you get the $65 a month combat pay for?"

Recon provided two squads of men for this mission, albeit at reduced strength due mostly to attrition. Their missions were inherently more dangerous than line troops because Recon had fewer troops to defend themselves; participation was voluntary. Among their men on this operation were a Vietnamese tiger scout, a new member who had just joined, and experienced Recon members.

A "Tango" armored troop carrier
(public domain photo)

The brief enemy attack had no major effect on the boats or the mission, but it could be seen to portend a *bad moon* warning. It was thought to be predictive by one of the Recon platoon members who came to SGT Chapple and confessed, "I cannot go on a mission tonight because I feel I will be killed." Chapple counseled him that everyone gets that fear. "You just need to push through it. Besides, you are assigned to carry the aid bag and act as the medic for this squad if anyone gets hit." But later that night, when it was time to board the Tangos for the mission, the frightened man was a no-show. He forced the ambush team to leave without the squad's medic and their first aid bag.

We loaded up about three-quarters of the forty-men capacity to each boat and pushed off. It was a slow, several-hour ride at about five knots with the unavoidable noise from the Gray Marine 225-hp diesel engines signaling our approach to everyone from klicks away. Seating in the Tango landing craft was nonexistent, meaning we sat encapsulated in the boat's bottom on the naked hull itself with the high steel sides denying visibility to the passengers. The dull hum and steel hull vibration from the dual Tango motors put many of us to sleep. I had just, it seemed, taken off my web gear and shut my eyes.

We were awakened by a deafening blast and impact force at 00:10, ten minutes into my twenty-second birthday. My head was blown back hard against the steel hull, leaving me temporarily groggy and with reduced hearing acuity, partially because of the loud ringing in my ears. A 75 mm recoilless rifle shaped charge round had impacted our boat, apparently from the Tân Trụ side of the river, with more than enough kinetic energy imparted by the projectile to sink us. The 75 mm round hit the higher side of the Tango above the waterline. It blew a large hole in it, on the port side of the boat, spraying shrapnel over the troops huddled below.

The 75 mm recoilless rifle used in the ambush against us

We were the second boat of two, the proper target by an experienced enemy. As they no doubt understood, by shooting at the second in line, the first boat, taking time to realize what had happened, would have passed on down the river. In its movement away from the enemy, the first Tango could not easily turn and fire on them.

The impact had a devastating result. At least twenty-seven men on the second Tango caught shrapnel, with seven dead among us. Captain Ray Smith, whose tour was almost over, was not hurt. I felt sure it wounded me because as I stood up, I could feel a stinging impact and wetness on my head, face, and left shin. As I turned my body back around, my eyes could barely resolve the form of a Vietnamese soldier who had been sitting shoulder-to-shoulder with me. He had taken a fatal hit to his head and face.

The impact on my shin did not affect my ability to walk; it was probably a shrapnel flesh wound, I reasoned. That one could wait to treat. There was immediate action to take.

The near moonless night was eerily quiet as a flashlight panned through the blackness and over the still figures to assess the damage. The smell of gunpowder and sweet, metallic, syrupy blood was overpowering. Ray Smith, the soft-spoken, experienced infantry captain, uttered in a dumbfounded voice as his flashlight revealed the extent of the tragedy in front of him, "Oh my God."

As our boat briefly sat adrift in the still water near where the shell had hit us, I remember saying in a rather excited voice to him, "Sir, we've got to get out of here!" I knew that the first boat had continued downriver, and we sat motors off and unmoved, easy prey to another

Captain Ray Smith, Infantry

31

artillery round with no one in a position to bring fire on the enemy. Captain Smith smiled at this young second lieutenant and reached the boat pilot on the radio. They confirmed which side of the river was our home district. Without further attack, we coordinated with the other Tango boat. They came alongside, tied up to us, and we made our way out of the kill zone to the Tân Trụ side of the river. As the drop-down ramp released to the brackish riverbank, a third odor entered the mix. The smell was well-known to soldiers of the Mekong Delta, that of riverine mud, mangrove, and decomposing vegetation.

We disembarked, carrying the dead and wounded onto Việt Cộng-controlled territory of Nhựt Ninh village, setting up a defensive perimeter and calling for battlefield illumination and medical helicopter dustoffs. Waiting my turn to offload from the boat, I felt my face and fatigues again and realized it was not *my* wound. I was handling marble-sized chunks of another person that had splattered me. The sting on my left shin continued, though, all but confirming a minor shrapnel wound. And I was still somewhat dizzy from the blast trauma.

I was one of the last to step onto shore and came face-to-face with two stacks of three and four stretchers holding apparently dead men. They were friendly Vietnamese soldiers who were part of tonight's operation, stacked off to the side on the mud bank. SGT Ken Chapple, who had inquired about my rank the previous evening, was seriously wounded.

As he later recounted to me, SGT Chapple knew he was critically wounded and losing blood quickly. His hand was shot through and through by shrapnel with six body wounds including his shoulder, left wrist, both legs, left forearm, and the left side of his face. Ken staggered as he fought to stand up from his position deep in the Tango boat, but his legs gave out and he fell back toward the opposite side. Then, remembering his religious teaching, he recited a prayer, but it left him feeling hollow. As Ken was lying there waiting to die, he stared toward the front of the boat.

The sight was surreal. Running down the middle of the boat hull among the tangle of dead and wounded men was what he described as a *river of blood*. He thought he was going to die and prayed in his own words, asking for God's acceptance of his soul. That was the ticket—an immediate sense of calm came over him.

Even though the evening weather was humid, Ken Chapple could feel the cold setting in from his body's loss of blood. He was bleeding out and had to be attended to quickly or he would become a casualty. Ken saw CPT Smith and asked him for his aid bag, but Ray Smith, like I, carried only our personal bandages. Ken resorted to immediate action, applying manual direct pressure on his wrist wound. The Recon medic from the other Tango could finally treat him after reaching him on our boat.

The first *dustoff* chopper arrived at 00:35 to evacuate the wounded and drop off stretchers to litter-carry those who could not walk. They loaded all the ambulatory wounded that their helicopter weight limit allowed and quickly ferried them back to base camp. They returned for the stretchered wounded, including SGT Chapple and other Recon soldiers who by now were prepped for evacuation. A second medevac helicopter came in directly after the first.

I climbed a few steps up the mud-slippery riverbank into a rice paddy and noticed a Vietnamese soldier standing there hunched over. As I approached him, he turned toward me, revealing how badly this man needed evacuation.

The twenty-two-year-old was carrying his weapon, an M79 grenade launcher in one hand and many loops of his intestines with his other arm. He held his exposed colon closely against his body as I helped him up into the medevac helicopter, its main rotor already turning at near liftoff speed. He sat and edged his body left and right, sidling backward, eventually reaching an open space on the chopper floor, and then handed me his sticky blood-soaked weapon. In one of the strangest visuals I had during my entire tour, *he looked up and smiled at me.* The chopper rose about ten feet, nodded forward, and was gone.

I think this man knew he was out of the war from then on, the war he had known his entire life. The chopper would get him medical attention in time. He would survive this wound to live a less conscripted existence. Weeks later, when I asked Intel Sergeant "P" about this man's condition, I was told of his permanent injury. "He's okay, but when he shits, he doesn't know."

At about this time, SGT Chapple, still on the boat, was put on a stretcher and carried out. As the men were lugging him up the river-bank in the yet unilluminated area, the man toting the stretcher's front end slipped and fell, accidentally kicking Ken Chapple severely in the head. They picked Ken up and took him over to the first chopper that had returned from the base camp after the drop-off of the walking wounded. He waited while lying on his stretcher in the rice paddy to be loaded onto the medevac chopper. Perhaps to keep Chapple's mind active or due to his nervousness in seeing Ken's condition, another man from Recon asked Ken for a cigarette, which he was in no condition to supply.

The dustoff chopper was so loaded with stretchered wounded that Ken was placed at the last position up high in a darkened area just below the chopper ceiling. During the ride to the US Army's 3rd Field Hospital in Sài Gòn, the helicopter's engine sputtered. Ken was wondering why so many things appeared to be going successively wrong.

Sergeant Ken Chapple, Recon Platoon, 2/60 (photo courtesy K. Chapple)

After the hurried chopper landing in Sài Gòn, the wounded were quickly off-loaded and carried into the emergency room area where treatment could begin. All except SGT Chapple who, because of the unusual placement of his stretcher on the medevac helicopter for crowding, was overlooked.

He lay there in the quiet darkened area next to the ceiling, immobile. *I'm not going to make it*, he thought, and the weak body movements he could muster only amounted to a squishing sound from his blood profusion saturating the stretcher. He could feel the life draining out of him as his body tried to keep what blood he still had in his system pumping through his body core. *He realized they had forgotten him.*

Many things were going wrong after the wounding. He was nearly convinced he would not survive. Inside the hospital, one of his less seriously wounded buddies asked, "Where's Chapple?" A quick check among those receiving treatment did not account for Ken. Realizing then that Chapple must still be on the chopper, some of the crew ran back to retrieve him. Ken heard footsteps. "There he is! There he is!" They pulled his stretcher off the helicopter. He was nearly lifeless by this time as they finally brought him in for emergency care.

But the ER nurse could not get an IV bloodline in SGT Chapple. After failing to find a suitable vein even in his ankle and seeing his deteriorating condition, she called for a doctor twice before finally demanding to a physician, "Doctor, you need to come here now!" Seeking a positive identification, confirming the name on his American camo fatigue shirt, before administering the proper blood type, the nurse asked, "Is your name really Chapple?" And he was all but unconscious but aware enough to reply in the affirmative and feel the warmth of the blood coming back into his body. He thought of the *river of blood* he witnessed in the Tango boat and now an hour later felt a *river of life* coursing through him—with enough blood now in his body to start his wounds bleeding again.

"Are you allergic to anything?" The response from Ken, clearly feeling life again, was, "Yes, shrapnel." As the medical team began the surgery, Ken asked the doctor to save his left hand, and the reply was pure SOP. "If we can, we will." And they could do exactly that. But the extent of the wounds left him with a permanent hand injury and no sensation in two of his fingers.

SGT Ken Chapple survived and recovered from his wounds, but his fighting days in Viêt Nam were over. He transferred to the Army 249th General Hospital in Japan for two weeks, then back stateside to Fitzsimmons Army Hospital in Colorado. Ken's time in the military was extended for two months. He needed two more surgeries on his hand to repair the snapped forearm ulna bone and more fully recover under their care.

He would finish his military time and become a police officer in the City of Madera, California, for eleven years, then to Clovis, California where an assailant shot him in the arm in the line of duty. Ken's law enforcement career ended with an on-the-job traffic accident; he sustained a broken neck. He medically retired in 2006.

As we later learned, once again someone had alerted the Viêt Cộng we were coming to Nhựt Ninh village by boat that evening. Their "loose lips" occurred in the local marketplace, as the word was passed to the Viêt Cộng, underscoring the villager sympathy and support for the enemy. The ambushers had become the ambush targets, and the Vietnamese district chief vowed to never again use Tango boats as troop transports or assault watercraft.

A few days later, Captain Smith and I drove our Jeep to Sài Gòn to visit my Phoenix counterpart in the Vietnamese hospital. He was a student officer, new to the military, an Aspirant (Chuẩn úy) in

*The Tân Trụ marketplace where a Vietnamese soldier
carelessly mentioned our planned ambush.*

the local Vietnamese popular force on his first combat mission. The enemy wounded him in three places, breaking his elbow. He was sheepish in seeing us, probably remembering his focus on himself, running through the Tango boat after the artillery shell hit, holding his arm, and loudly seeking medical attention. He had been afraid, as were we all. It was something more experienced soldiers had learned to hide.

Driving through Sài Gòn to our next stop, the sight of a striking blond American woman amazed us. She stood on a corner in a sea of dark-haired Vietnamese. Captain Smith wheeled a U-turn, and we stopped to give her a lift. She quietly identified herself as the private secretary to General Creighton Abrams, Commander, US Military Assistance Command (COMUSMACV). Her contention may have been true; she asked to be dropped off at MACV headquarters.

Since we were in the area and rarely got to Sài Gòn, I stopped at III Corps headquarters, to see the new Phoenix Program III Corps CO, a full bird colonel. As we entered the facility, I met his second in command. He was skeptical that I was requesting only a bread-and-butter meeting. I was stopping in to welcome the CO, but his second was assuming an ulterior motive. He kept asking, before he would let me in to see the CO, what negative information I was trying to pass on to the colonel. Apparently, a few weeks earlier another second lieutenant visited ostensibly to greet the new CO and instead gave a complaint litany, blindsiding the second in command. I eventually got in to see the CO and enjoyed a brief welcome chat. On the way out, the second in command pulled me aside, apparently convinced I was genuine and perhaps a useful source for answers to district-level direct questions. He asked me how I handled the problem of my Vietnamese counterpart requesting personal supplies from the PX. I replied that for my counterpart, I did what I could, when I could. As he repeated that quote as I left, he seemed satisfied with my answer.

For the next month, I sat on my butt pushing paper, licking my psych wounds, and distracting myself with novel reading material. It did not help that I received a disap-pointing letter from the woman back in the World I cared the most about. I recall SFC Charles Jones, a team member, mentor, and unmatched mortarman telling me I looked like someone who had lost their best friend. Well, time to put on my game face and get back out there.

I got further jerked out of my funk by the visit of my brother George ("Chief") whose 3rd Marine Division had recently been pulled from the DMZ back to Okinawa. His appearance was a complete surprise even though I had casually suggested in a letter he come visit. Chief

George Loewer, USMC

told me later that the visit never would have happened if I had not been an officer.

I was out on an op when SFC Jones radioed to me "Your brother came in at Tân Sơn Nhứt (airport) and is on his way here." As Jones later told me he knew I was going to say it. I responded, "Say again?" SFC Jones assured he'd be pleased to pick up Chief at the Tân An airport and have him at our compound by the time I got back in from the field and cleaned up.

Chief and I took a few days and went to Vũng Tàu, a relatively safe beachside area in Việt Nam, for a brief R&R and it was well worth the trip. We ended up staying at the officer's club and writing a joint letter home. A diverting observation while we were at Tân Sơn Nhứt airport, waiting for the Air America hop to come in was the landing of a Lockheed U-2 Dragon Lady high-altitude reconnaissance aircraft. The U-2 does not have permanent wheels under the wings. It cannot stand without falling over, so it taxied off the runway and directly into a hangar.

Just after Thanksgiving, they presented the awards for heroism during the Nhựt Ninh village action. Although I was new to the task, I very much regretted not doing a better job writing up Captain Smith's award narrative. As the only other American officer on the operation, the task fell to me. Those who had more experience with this process recommended I put him in for a Bronze Star with "V" device for valor. Sadly, it was downgraded to an Army Commendation Medal with "V" device. The fact is Captain Ray Smith distinguished himself during that combat action and he was not fully recognized for it.

Six months later we captured the 75 mm recoilless rifle, three rounds of ammunition, a B40 rocket launcher with four grenades, and plastic explosives pictured here along with the two Việt Cộng who eventually led us to the weapon. They hid it underwater next

to a paddy dike. Before making the return trip after retrieving the weapon, we dressed them as ARVN soldiers to reduce their chances of being recognized and shot by other Việt Cộng. Was it satisfying to bring in that 75 mm RR with ammunition? You bet it was!

Chapter 5
The Phụng Hoàng (Phoenix) Warriors

The Phoenix program embraced fighters from both Vietnamese and American military units. American advisors were placed with Vietnamese elements such as the CIA-trained Provincial Reconnaissance Unit (PRU) paramilitary and hand-picked military from local forces. In my case, I was operating as a riceroots-level Phoenix advisor in the District Intelligence and Operations Coordinating Center, the base tactical level of the organization.

There were hundreds of districts within the aggregate of forty-four provinces of Viêt Nam, each district Phoenix force targeting the Viêt

Fourth in line on this Phoenix operation traversing
the foot bridge is SP5 John Mullenax, medic and RTO.

Cộng Infrastructure, the covert civilian government of COSVN. General Trần Độ, the enemy deputy commander of COSVN, commenting after the war, characterized Phoenix as "extremely destructive."

William E. Colby, the former CIA Sài Gòn Station chief, noted in 1972:

> Operation Phoenix was run not by the CIA but by the Government of Việt Nam, with the support of the CORDS element of the U.S. Military Assistance Command in coordination with several U.S. agencies including CIA. Operation Phoenix is not and was not a program of assassination. It countered the Việt Cộng apparatus attempting to overthrow the Government of Việt Nam by targeting its leaders. Wherever possible, these were apprehended or invited to defect, but a substantial number were killed in firefights during military operations or resisting capture. There is a vast difference in kind, not merely in degree, between these combat casualties, (even including the few abuses which occurred) and the victims of the Việt Cộng's systematic campaign of terrorism.

The Vietnamese Intel Squad

The Phoenix military in Tân Trụ operated out of the district government's rectangular compound, a small moat-encircled facility with little defense fortifications compared to American base camps. During the rainy season, the moat had a few feet of water over several feet of mud. On both the inner and outer perimeters of the moat, barbed wire was strung to an average height of about six feet, with small firing position bunker emplacements at two of the four corners. The compound's single, most effective defensive structure, however, was its tower. Near the center but placed closer to the advisor's hooch, it topped twenty-five feet, a wooden skeleton supporting the sandbagged guard housing at its crown. Vietnamese soldiers manned the tower through each night and often during the daytime. It supported an M60 machine gun, a high-powered searchlight, and a hand-cranked siren with a sound suggestive of a 1950s air raid alarm.

During each evening, Vietnamese troops would scan the perimeter with the searchlight and if they observed suspected or obvious enemy activity, two actions could occur. First, the hand-turned, wailing siren would sound out. Second, the men in the tower would respond with machine gun fire if they believed enemy might be present. As Americans living in the Vietnamese government compound, we were a more tempting strategic target than the US 2/60 base camp two klicks away. Tactically, we were much less formidable and less well defended both by manpower and weaponry. The district chief, a Vietnamese major, lived in the center of the compound in a less modest facility than others along with a large bunker—both housing him, his wife, and his two small children.

The sandbagged tower in the Tân Trụ compound.

The Phoenix force was hand-picked from locals—those who knew the area and its people well and was called the Intel Squad. Among its members were several former Việt Cộng. A company

My two officer counterparts during my tour. The aspirant on the left was wounded and later replaced by the lieutenant on the right.

grade officer commanded the unit, but many operations were undertaken with the more experienced sergeants in charge. American advisors often accompanied the Intel force into the field. We were useful in coordinating gunship and medevac support and asserting relevant intelligence reporting, and by suggesting the most effective ways of applying that support and information. When American units op'ed with us, such as the 2/60 Recon, I would act to ensure cohesion between the Vietnamese and American forces.

From left to right: "H", a former Việt Cộng and good friend; "P", the Intel NCO leader and Vietnamese I was closest to; and "S", my RTO and perennial jokester.

Photographs of Vietnamese in the field will often show some of them wearing red neck scarves, seemingly counterintuitive for a military operation where cover from enemy fire was important. The men would wear the scarves to reduce friendly fire mistakes when helicopter gunships saw them as targets of opportunity and fired erroneously on the wrong Vietnamese. Friendly fire accidents accounted for as much as twenty-five percent of casualties in wartime action.

Vietnamese troops wearing the red neck scarf.
Note the relatively wide spacing between the men.

As a powerful indicator of the competence of Intel during my tour, except for the ambush of August 15, we lost only one man from the Intel squad. He is pictured here and was killed on a Phoenix mission by booby trap in January 1970. An M-79 round set to trigger under water about waist high exploded as the man walked through a rivulet. He sustained extensive small caliber wounds to his chest suggestive of an M79 high explosive round that sprayed metal pellet-sized pieces. Despite prompt medical efforts by Recon platoon medic Bob Schnell, he did not survive the helicopter evacuation to the hospital.

A member of Intel, KIA by booby trap in early January 1970.
Note the four choppers in the distant background coming in for a pickup.

I occasionally heard comments from others, particularly chopper pilots and crews of their lack of interest in providing helicopter support for Vietnamese soldiers. They would point out that the Vietnamese troops appeared lackluster and unmotivated. There were times I saw main force Vietnamese unit behavior such that I would have to agree with their view. But I did not witness that with the Phoenix soldiers. These men, particularly the Intel warriors, were

My red neck scarf I wore occasionally in the
field with the Intel squad

hand-selected, motivated, and expert on the locale. I sometimes heard the crews from choppers we used affectionately refer to the Vietnamese as the "Little People."

An operation in the spring of 1970 sent the Intel squad, SP5 Mullenax—our medic, occasional RTO, and proud Appalachian native—and me about five klicks northeast of our compound well into the land area known as the elbow. We had intelligence on a few Việt Cộng, possibly members of the Việt Cộng Infrastructure, who were hiding in the nipa palm near a river.

As our force of Vietnamese Intel and their two advisors approached the nipa, we took enemy fire. We could not be certain of the size of the enemy force, so we called for helicopter gunship support. Within fifteen minutes the gunship arrived, having been part of a US operation a few klicks away that did not have an immediate need for the support firepower. Along with the rocket-equipped AH-1G Cobra came the Command and Control Huey with the US troop commander, eager to observe what their gunship asset was being used for and what they might accomplish.

The Cobra made several attack runs, pounding the estuary with 70 mm Mk 40 Folding Fin Aerial Rockets known as the Mighty Mouse, throwing up considerable amounts of dirt and mud. The Mighty Mouse was a good fit for slower-moving aircraft like choppers. It had a speed of a smoke-trailed 600 meters per second, making for a highly visible display. With the softening up of the target area, the Cobra withdrew, and we moved in on foot. We had reached the edge of the nipa palm when the enemy began firing sporadically at us. But then, more concentrated, bullets whizzing past as we approached. *Too much*, I thought. *We are going to be hit.* The team's interpreter, Sergeant "L", a solid, motivated man but by nature a non-fighter, exclaimed, "They are shooting at us!" "L" almost never went into the field but this time we reacted instinctively together.

He thrust his M16 toward the source of the automatic weapons fire and shot back vigorously.

A handful of our men advanced into the nipa thicket, attacked, and quickly ended the firefight, capturing one and killing two Việt Cộng. One of the dead enemies was female. Her body was dragged into the clearing. A former Việt Cộng member of Intel, whom I regarded as a walking aberration and little more than an out-and-out killer, moved toward her. He removed the woman's black pajama bottoms and shot her naked vagina while laughing. It was a sad thing to see and while only momentary, the image of that depravity stayed with me for months.

Shortly after, the Command and Control chopper was nosing over the nipa, perhaps thirty feet off the ground. The pilot foolishly entered the area just above the Vietnamese troops as they were mopping up when one member of Intel shot into the air to announce his exhilaration at the success of the operation. With the same sense men know with great accuracy where an arcing baseball is going to come down, I knew an imminent collision between the helicopter and the 5.56 mm ammunition from where his M16 was shooting, set to semiautomatic fire, was about to happen. I quickly raised my arms, vigorously pushing the chopper back through the air as if I could control it. But as bad as the scene was looking, good fortune visited us this day. The pilot saw me gesturing and immediately pulled back on his stick, practically standing the chopper on its tail, barely feet off the top of the nipa palm.

It must have been a rude experience for the senior officers on the helicopter. Within a few seconds, one of them with an older voice, presumably a senior field grade officer, remarked, "Control those people!" It was an abrupt response to an unexpected event. I ignored it, of course, but understood the gravity of what almost happened and the officer's exasperation. If he had any experience with combat situations from the ground, however, he would know that on occasion, particularly after a firefight where death was cheated by the victors, discipline can go out the window. You cannot control the celebratory atmosphere. In such situations, I sought to settle for applying influence as experienced advisors were wont to do.

As we milled around, waiting for the Command and Control helicopter to depart, a sampan appeared on the meandering estuarial stream nearby, moving toward our number. A member of Intel called my attention to the craft and told the piloting papa san to give Thiếu úy Mỹ (me) a glass-bottled Coca-Cola from one of the cases of twenty-four on board. I considered this a real treat. We were hot and sweaty, and the sugary drink would go down easily. I accepted the soda quickly. To do less would have been rude.

The papa san uncapped the bottle and passed it to me. I drank it appreciatively and idly, standing among the men, held onto the bottle. One man asked me for the bottle back. I joked *no*, which brought a round of laughter from some Intel men. But the sampan did not continue his journey, and it was then that I realized, to these people, the six-ounce Coca-Cola glass bottle was worth much more than the cola itself. I returned the bottle. Wow. Another example of regional differences between life in rural Việt Nam and the United States.

We captured two unusual items in this enemy encounter, a Chicom type 56 light machine gun and an unidentified Chicom radio. The radio's appearance was PRC-25 size but about half the thickness. It was a dark amber color with an amber glass vial filled with a powder as an antenna.

On the walk back to the district compound, Bác sĩ, our medic, appeared upset, feeling frustrated that we had not done a field interrogation of the captured man, a suspected member of the VCI. Bác sĩ knew that interrogations by Intel in the field immediately after both sides being subjected to each other's fire could provide more information than a less intense questioning at our compound. The field grilling was bypassed because of the presence of the Command and Control chopper, likely carrying three or more field grade US officers and who, from their vantage point, could witness all that took place. While the field interrogations were not inhumane or illegal, they could be edgy, and were not something any advisor would want to have to explain to potentially embarrassed senior US officers from another unit.

A portion of Bác sĩ Mullenax's conversation with me, as we trekked the five klicks back through the paddy mud and across the dikes, went something like this:

Mullenax: *So, are we supposed to ignore that these VC shot at us? You know what they would do to us if it were turned around. Why didn't we interrogate them?*

Me: *We'll do it back at the compound, Bác sĩ. Here everyone can see what is going on.*

Mullenax: *And so, we not only must obey the [Geneva] rules, but now we have to worry about what other Americans think?*

Me: *Those in the Command and Control ship don't go out into the field with us, Bác sĩ. They don't know what it's like. They don't see what we see.*

Mullenax: *(After a pause...) Oh. I understand, sir.*

Me: *(Silence.)*

Mullenax: *I understand, sir!*

Me: *(Silence.)*

Somehow, I hit the nail on the head with Bác sĩ. I had gone up a notch with him in the trust department. And it advanced even further on another operation when he, acting as RTO and humping the PRC-25 radio, got bogged down in a ditch as we were briefly isolated from the other men. Enemy were in the area. I had to put

my M-16 down, which I never did, and leave both of us unde-
fended. I placed my weapon on the muddy terrain and used my full
strength with both arms. It was as if I were performing the Heimlich
maneuver, pulling him up and out of two feet of mud. The process
was made difficult because his boots, buried deep in the mud, acted
as suction cups, keeping him trapped. Air could not enter the rising
boot space deep in the mud, making a vacuum pulling against us
as I levered him up.

I went through a period of craziness about halfway through my
tour when my tactical competence had geared up to running full
bore. I thought I was unlikely to become a casualty in this war, and
I took unnecessary risks. Two examples come to mind. I thoroughly
enjoyed daytime helicopter insertion flights when those assets were
used in an operation. I felt prepared for anything, landing in a rice
paddy, often facing a strip of nipa palm. As the choppers approached
the ground, I would let myself slide out and off the floor down to
the landing skid. I stood on it, outside of the chopper, as the pilot
set the craft down. Incredibly exhilarating and stupid.

A different operation had us approach a large patch of nipa
immediately after insertion. We were about six men from Intel,
me, and my RTO. We had casually formed a line, well separated,
and moved deliberately forward in that fashion. Within seconds
of walking toward the nipa, weapons at the hilt, my RTO told me
Major Gravett was on the horn and wanted to talk to me. Gravett was
above us in the C&C ship. I responded to him with my call sign, and
he calmly said, "Just remember, you are not in charge down there."
Not at all what I wanted to hear as we were moving in on the nipa!
I thrust the handset away from my head, stiff-arming it to my RTO,
without responding to the major. He was right, of course, and was
looking out for me. But I did not want to be told that.

Seemingly untouched by war, moats could
hide underwater entrances to bunkers.

On another occasion later in my tour, an event that touches on some less comfortable aspects of human behavior occurred. It illustrated how we as people will use methods to reach goals that can be considered inappropriate. In this case, it involved children. But it was *war*.

We were seeking two VCI who, based on our Phoenix Program intelligence, were reported to frequent a certain area in a remote hamlet. It was not uncommon for the local enemy to live close to their family home, sometimes staying in a nearby hidden bunker and emerging only under the cover of darkness to visit their kin and carry out their duties.

We believed they were in a bunker dug deeply in a pond mud bank, not unlike that shown in the photo. Once we arrived at the hut in question, my Vietnamese counterpart talked to two young children who unwittingly gave clues to the location of the underground bunker. A careful search of the place identified by the children soon

The ejecta of a green M18 smoke grenade.
Public domain photo.

revealed a well-camouflaged ventilation shaft leading down into the ground.

We grabbed an M18 red smoke grenade, a canister device used primarily for signaling, pointed the business end of the grenade into the bunker air duct, and released it. Vast amounts of smoke went down the airway and shortly thereafter, reddish bubbles came up in the pond water, revealing the proximate underwater entrance to the bunker.

> **Smoke grenades** were often used to help helicopter pilots correctly identify the landing site and avoid an enemy trap. For example, when helicopters would arrive "on station" to pick up troops, they would identify themselves over the radio and advise the men on the ground to "pop smoke." The troops would pick from the smoke grenade colors they carried (red, yellow, green, violet), pull the pin on the smoke canister, and toss it downwind. When released, it would make a sharp popping sound and produce billows of brightly colored, somewhat toxic smoke. The ground troops would announce over the radio "smoke popped"—without naming the color. The pilot would then counter with "I see (e.g., yellow) smoke," confirming that his sighting was the intended location.

Within a minute, two Việt Cộng appeared in the water, spitting out the red aerosolized powder. They were disoriented and immediately captured, no shots fired, and no friendly casualties. When asked, I estimated these enemy soldiers, given the amount of toxic particulate they inhaled, would probably not live long. We took them without incident, alive and available for interrogation.

It was an ingenious tactic. I loved serving with these experienced and knowledgeable Vietnamese soldiers. Their average age was twenty-six. To a man, they had not seen peace in their homeland.

The US Recon Platoon

In the book *In the Land of Nine Dragons*, David Argabright and Robert Vargas, editors, relate through a comprehensive retelling of the history of the 2/60 during its time in Tân Trụ, the impressively substantial fortifications of the battalion base camp.

> … a six-to-ten-foot-high berm of dirt accented every hundred yards or so by bunkers. …we constructed our bunkers by building up layers of sandbags, topped with 12 x 12s, corrugated metal sheeting and more sandbags. Each had about an 8x48 inch gun slit facing out and was fronted by a makeshift metal fencing contraption that looked something like a little league baseball backstop.

While quartered in then Việt Cộng-controlled territory since 1967, there was inherent safety for personnel in their battalion strength numbers and their fortifications. Anything less for a permanently stationed US unit was unacceptable. This was Battalion Headquarters; this was Camp Scott. The sheer size, armament, and ability to bring firepower at will on the enemy was a highly effective deterrent to any ground attack from local Việt Cộng and NVA battalions. And the enemy saw it as so.

During its entire three-year residency in Tân Trụ, the 2/60 was subjected to just one ground attack. It was quickly repulsed. The enemy never crossed the battalion perimeter wire. The substantial fortifications were necessary defenses for the American battalion as 2/60 platoon leader Lieutenant Joseph Callaway, Jr. noted in his book, *Mekong First Light*. He also knew that the Tân Trụ "boonies" as he called them, thinly populated or unsettled nipa-peppered rural areas, could be exceedingly dangerous. His example in Tân Trụ was the region known as the testicles, five-to-six klicks south of the 2/60 base camp and our district compound.

In their Tân Trụ area of operation, from the testicles to the elbow to the bowling alley, Callaway and the men of his platoon well understood the enemy activity and proper home base defenses to it. But in contrast with the fortifications of the 2/60's solid footing, the Vietnamese district compound where advisors lived was, frankly, much more vulnerable to enemy attack. The berm was nonexistent on three sides; the moat was shallow and narrow, and the totality of defensive armament was a towered searchlight, an M-60 machine gun, and a hand-cranked wailing siren. Nonetheless, both installations were equally at risk for aerial mortar and rocket attacks, which occurred from time-to-time.

During its time in Tân Trụ, the 2/60 experienced significant enemy interactions within the district. This battalion was one of the most heavily casualtied and highly decorated of the war. Operations of the 2/60 also took place beyond the borders of Tân Trụ in even more remote locations. Across all platoons, enemy contact on operations was a near daily occurrence.

The Recon platoon and their larger organization, Company "E" of the 2/60, kept busy during their time. When they were not performing the basic combat reconnaissance mission with Vietnamese district and regional forces, the PRU or others, they could be found clearing mines from Tân Trụ's Thunder Road. Called the Road Runners, at 07:15 each morning they were clearing the twelve klicks of Road 225 west to the Tân Trụ boundary of Highway 4.

The US Army Field Manual 7-92 defines the role of the Recon platoon:

> The infantry reconnaissance platoon is a specialty platoon comprising infantry soldiers. Unlike traditional infantry platoons whose primary mission is to kill the enemy, the reconnaissance platoon's primary mission is to provide the battalion commander information about the enemy. The battalion commander uses the reconnaissance platoon to gather critical battlefield information. This information is used by the commander and his staff during the planning and execution of combat operations.

The Recon platoon of Company E was no exception. Their area of operation extended beyond the boundaries of Tân Trụ and its Vietnamese Intel squad, both in the geographic area of operation and type of force they worked with. For Recon, Phoenix was but one of their missions.

When First Lieutenant Jeff Riek rotated in as Recon platoon leader, he was replacing First Lieutenant Ron Pieper, an experienced and well-liked officer coming off six months commanding Recon. During Pieper's tour, I had gotten to know him somewhat. That friendship grew when we encountered each other a year or so later stateside at Fort Belvoir, Virginia.

Jeff Riek's and my friendship, in contrast, advanced rather slowly. Jeff was a highly competitive man and quite a jokester. He was immensely proud, like many of his men, of his assignment to the all-volunteer Recon platoon. Over the following couple of months, a rapport developed, and he suggested we go on R&R together in Sydney, Australia. The idea appealed to me. We were just getting to know one another. Since we were op'ing together with our respective units, I wanted to know him better, and visiting another country was always more appealing with two. We were both thinking about a May timeframe so it might work out.

But sadly, it was not to be. I had intelligence on an area in Tân Trụ from which I normally did not receive reports of enemy activity. We put an operation together for the next morning, February 25, 1970, with men from both Intel and Recon. Jeff Riek was commanding, and I would accompany Intel since I was their advisor. As fate sometimes deals in unanticipated ways, I was informed the night before I would brief a visitor the following morning, meaning I would not be going on the operation. No biggie: that happened from time-to-time. Going into the field was not my primary mission, I was occasionally reminded. Keeping Phoenix in Tân Trụ district moving along was the mission.

On the next day's combined forces operation, the men came under mid-morning fire shortly after entering a clearing in a large thicket of nipa palm. One of the Intel men had noticed fresh feces. When he voiced what he had found, enemy gunfire from the nipa palm immediately arose. Jeff Riek and Bob Mossgrove, his RTO, were struck on the first volley by small arms fire and died within minutes. Gunship help was called in and by the afternoon, helicopter-fired 70 mm Mighty Mouse rockets had destroyed the entire nipa line. Many secondary explosions appeared during the gunship attack, revealing stored munitions. When it was over, seventeen enemy bodies—mostly Việt Cộng and a few NVA—were removed. We do not know how many bodies the rockets destroyed and were thus unrecognizable and uncountable.

It is noteworthy that people native to North Việt Nam are built heavier than those from the south. And aside from the clothes they were wearing, which was not always a reliable way to tell NVA from Việt Cộng, we could know with reasonable certainty which of the dead were NVA by observing the corpse's disposition. The bodies of those from the north often went unburied by the locals, showing strong animosity from Việt Cộng families toward the members of the North Vietnamese Army. A day after this firefight, several of the enemy bodies were recognized as NVA because their corpses went unclaimed and unburied by any local family.

On the afternoon of the Recon loss, I slowly steered my jeep to the 2/60 base camp to learn more of what had happened from the American viewpoint. As I arrived, the CO, a taciturn LTC William Ciccolo, who had earned a reputation for being tough on subordinates, was walking across a parking area. He pivoted toward me and was trying awfully hard to conceal how upset he was. He brought up his hand in an offer to receive a salute from me, and I quickly matched his gesture.

He remarked with a heavy brow, "Lieutenant Loewer, we're going to get another Recon platoon leader right away." The man

BG Camp and 1LT Jeff Riek. At the far left is LTC Ciccolo, 2/60 Battalion commander. (public domain photo)

was consoling me by affirming his belief in the CRIP mission and declaring operations would continue with no unnecessary delay. LTC Ciccolo was not an officer at ease, feeling the weight of his command and his consequent need to assert authority. This expression of emotion surprised me, but his assurances were precise and directed, exactly what was called for and appreciated. LTC Ciccolo's grief for 1LT Jeff Riek showed him to be as vulnerable and as resolute a soldier as the rest of his battalion.

A few days later, the 2/60 held a memorial service for both Jeff Riek and Bob Mossgrove. At the appointed time, I invited and took with me about a half-dozen members of Intel who, while they did not know Lieutenant Riek or Specialist Mossgrove personally, had great respect for him and fellow combatants from Recon. The Vietnamese took the deaths of Americans they worked with in defense of their country with more sorrow than many GIs realized.

As we took our places in the ceremonial formation, I could see the inverted rifles, boots, and Recon berets belonging to Jeff and Bob. Off to the side and out of view of the Intel men standing at attention, was the honor guard about to fire a three-volley salute to the fallen men. In a move to prevent the Intel men from being surprised by the sudden close gunfire at this solemn ceremony unfamiliar to them, I whispered to the Intel group "Whang-O," a Vietnamese contortion of the American *fire-in-the-hole*, used to alert to an imminent friendly explosion nearby. Some men flinched, but mostly the warning helped.

Here is pictured, weeks before his death, Recon platoon leader First Lieutenant Jeff Riek, mugging for my camera. Jeff was a West Pointer from a Falls Church, Virginia military family. His older brother was an army captain, his father an army lieutenant colonel who took Jeff's death with difficulty.

A few weeks after my return from Viêt Nam, I visited Jeff's family at their home in Falls Church. In doing so, I broke a few of the rules of societal politeness—I did not telephone the Rieks to ask if I could come by. I was certain they would want to talk with me. I had a first-hand account of their son's activities, and slides of their son pictured here to give them. But I was uncertain whether I could go through with it.

In what I regarded as the most difficult thing I had done in my life, I showed up on their doorstep unannounced on a balmy Virginia Sunday morning in khakis, complete with my combat fruit salad. The medals gave me the credibility to talk with them as an officer who had experienced combat with their son. In talking with Jeff's father, Lieutenant Colonel Riek, his mother Ruth, and his sister Bunny, I learned about this military family and the contribution they had made to America.

This was a family of proud West Pointers serving our country who had six months earlier, in Jeff's death, given the ultimate in service to our country. LTC Justus Riek was by nature a gruff man, and at this point beside himself with anger. He believed

the Vietnamese Tân Trụ district chief set up his son for ambush, inexplicably given this idea from a visiting member of the Recon platoon. LTC Riek wanted to take revenge and made the point that the wearing of red scarves by some members of Intel was suspicious. He had to have an explanation. So, as the only American who worked and lived with the Vietnamese who were present when his son died, I gave it to him.

I explained what the red scarves were for—to dissuade helicopter gunship pilots hundreds of feet in the air from shooting friendly force Vietnamese. I helped him appreciate that the district chief, a Vietnamese major with a great deal of power in Tân Trụ, was not a member of the Việt Cộng. He was visibly angry over this possibility, perhaps bitter about this belief, incorrect as it was. For the first time

1LT Jeff Riek (L) and SP4 Bob Mossgrove

in my military career, my awards and medals—the fruit salad—had a truly useful function. The Purple Heart, the Combat Infantry Badge, the others, all delivered instant credibility to my explanation, hopefully with convincing and possibly comforting words.

As I was leaving their house, LTC Riek walked me out to my car. During the visit he had showed uncertainty about precisely how his son had died. Out of earshot of his daughter and wife, I told him what he needed to hear. Over the next year I occasionally crossed paths with LTC Riek at the Pentagon, where we were both assigned. He was cordial but not friendly. I sensed his residual anger about Jeff's death and judged that seeing me was a reminder of that tragedy. I learned years later after his passing in 1974 that this deservedly proud man whose family had given so much in service to our country did not fully recuperate from the loss of his youngest son.

https://www.virtualwall.org/dr/RiekJR01a.htm

Jeff's RTO, SP4 Bob Mossgrove of Wellsburg, West Virginia, was also killed in the action. Since Bob's family was some travel distance from me, I wrote a letter to his family instead of a personal visit. His mother wrote back a heartfelt letter about Bob and his father, shown here, who at the time of her writing, was in poor health. As she agreed with me, Bob's family believed he had a sixth sense about things. He was immensely proud to be a member of the elite Recon platoon of the 2/60. As expected, Bob's death was taken hard by both of his parents.

https://www.virtualwall.org/dm/MossgroveRB01a.htm

3.

He said and did many things before going over there.

Bob's father is in the hospital and has been since May. He took ill about the time we received the word of Bob's death. He will never get over it he is seventy years old and they had so much in common, such as their guns and hunting.

This picture you are sending us will be treasured by us as we did not get any of Bob's very personal articles such as camera, knife, radio, religious medal and many other things which we had sent him. A formal investigation was held, but no trace of these could be found in fact they informed us that he did not own such things. We knew

4.

better because we sent them and he wrote and told us he received them.

Again I thank you for writing to us, and want you to know that it was one of the nicest things that has happened to us. You must be a wonderful person and I wish you the best of everything, and may God Bless you always.

I can hardly wait to get our son's photo and in return would like for you to have this picture of him. It is a print of the last picture he sent home. He was so proud of this uniform, especially the Beret. We rec'd. it Tues. and the following Fri. were told of his death.

Most Sincerely

Mrs. R.C. Mossgrove.

CRIP — The Combined Recon and Intel Platoon

Here are pictured some men in the Tân Trụ CRIP platoon — the amalgam of Vietnamese Intel and American Recon men. This photo shows an informal command hand-off, a meet-the-new-Recon-Platoon-Leader get-together. First Lieutenant Ron Pieper

From the left, three men of Recon: SGT Gibson, 1LT Ron Pieper,
1LT Jeff Riek. To the far right, advisor, and medic SP5 John Mullenax.

had completed his six months in the field and was passing the 2/60 Recon platoon leader, and hence CRIP platoon leader, responsibilities to First Lieutenant Jeff Riek. This CRIP operated in Tân Trụ with intelligence from Phoenix and other sources. It specialized as a joint rapid reaction force and was widely regarded as extremely effective.

The CRIP concept was first implemented in early 1967 at the 25th Infantry Division by combining a Vietnamese Regional Force intelligence platoon and a US reconnaissance platoon. The successes of this merger quickly begat similar entities across Việt Nam with

The photo shows the makeshift bunker just inside the housing area where the 70 mm Mighty Mouse rocket boxes are visible behind the men. Once these helicopter rockets were removed for use from their shipping containers, the boxes became salvage and were filled with dirt or sand and stacked up to five or six feet high to stop or reduce the blast energy of shrapnel from incoming mortar or rocket attacks.

equal successes. In our area of operation, Phoenix combined force operations were commonplace. During the second half of 1969, First Lieutenant Ron Pieper, commanding the 2/60 Reconnaissance platoon, either lent men to Phoenix ops or participated directly. In late 1969, First Lieutenant Jeff Riek rotated into the Reconnaissance platoon leader slot and began both Recon-only as well as CRIP operations.

Respect for the men of the Vietnamese Intel squad and the US Recon platoon was well-earned, and while no one enjoyed being shot at, I found in myself a deep simpatico with these men. While Phoenix intelligence officers were discouraged from going on operations, I came to achieve a special sense of purpose by doing exactly that.

Taking a break with the Intel squad.

While I was at it, I broke another rule while going into the field with only the Phoenix Intel men—I was the only American with them. Two of their number would trade off being my RTO. They spoke little to no English but could recognize my call sign. When they heard it—for example, *Rusty Scupper two-six-two*—they would alert me to the incoming call in broken English: *Two-sic-two*, they emphasized, pushing the handset in my direction. In our area of operation, call signs changed monthly for security reasons. In this example, our district advisory group was known as *Rusty Scupper two-six*. As the intelligence officer, a *two* was appended yielding *Rusty Scupper two-six-two*.

Though First Lieutenant Jeff Riek's time with Recon was but a few months, they credited him with resurrecting and using *stay-behind* or *leave-back* operations. It worked like this: they inserted a CRIP platoon in a nighttime Việt Cộng-controlled area a few hours before dark. The men would act as if on a raid, but with no apparent success. They would end the exercise and either get a chopper extraction or walk back at dusk to their base camps. Unknown to anyone watching, however, the CRIP would leave back two or three men hiding in one of the rural huts. As it darkened into evening, Việt Cộng would emerge and walk along the paddy dikes to affect their business. In response, the Recon and Intel men would stand and deliver, frequently killing or wounding the targets. The operations were extraordinarily successful but at greater risk to the men since nighttime maneuvering and walking back through Việt Cộng territory at night were inherently dangerous.

When the nature of the operation permitted, we would break from the Mekong weather at a selected straw hut of a citizen, buy a duck, and sit down for lunch. On the menu was usually *phở* (pronounced "fuh"), the Vietnamese national soup dish of meat with spicy vegetables. One afternoon, the Intel CO chose the hut of a family that had pigs and ducks. The Vietnamese men had purchased a duck from the owner for our lunch—duck soup—and began the preparation process.

They defeathered the duck and slit its neck at an artery, catching the blood in a bowl. The blood was prepared later; heated, cooled, and cut up into slices and served as part of lunch. It was a Mekong variant of Việt Nam's blood pudding known as *tiết canh vịt*. The "best" parts of the duck were placed in the soup pot, including some internal organs, usually gizzard and heart. My first time out with Intel was memorable. When lunch was in order, they gave me a soup bowl of duck meat and rice with the duck heart at the surface peering up at me, superior vena cava and all.

While cooking was underway, some men had taken off their ammo belts and were winding down for a breather away from the scorching sun and high humidity weather of the Mekong. Suddenly, there was an explosion near the hut and we quickly brought weapons to bear as we sought to investigate what had happened. There was not much remaining of one pig who had been rooting around the belts of our equipment unnoticed, placed near the outside walls of the hut. Apparently, one of the pigs had nosed over a baseball grenade and pulled the pin.

The explosion lightly wounded several of the Intel soldiers, but only the curious pig had suffered major wounds. Following proper procedure, our RTO radioed in the event reporting three VN (Vietnamese) WIA and one PIG KIA. No US casualties.

> The M76 fragmentation grenade has a spheroidal steel body that weighs about 14 ounces. It is easily thrown like a baseball, hence the nickname *baseball grenade*. After four to five seconds, it explodes, broadcasting many steel fragments at high velocity. The grenade's kill radius is about five meters.

The more we fought, the more we sought opportunities for laughter. And the Vietnamese loved to celebrate when the tactical situation allowed. Here is pictured the lunch pause on a CRIP operation. The two Vietnamese smiling at us are "M" and "S", who switched off

being my RTO. Behind them and mostly obscured are four men from the US Recon platoon. From left to right, the US men are #1 and #3 obscured, #2 First Lieutenant Jeff Riek partially obscured (KIA about a month later), and #4 an unidentified member of Recon.

Chapter 6

Hearts and Minds

rab 'em by the balls and their hearts and minds will follow. This was
G the popular American refrain spoken throughout most of the
war. Some regarded it as endorsed military policy, however, that was
directed toward the Vietnamese people who were ambivalent toward
the Việt Cộng. It was a phrase asserting a belief in the compelling
need for application of US military might instead of programs to
enjoin the rural citizenry away from North Vietnamese communist
influence and collaboration.

A seminal book on counterinsurgency, *Defeating Communist
Insurgency: The Lessons of Malaya and Vietnam*, written by the
highly respected Sir Robert Thompson and first published in 1966,
emphasized the criticality of securing the population. He eschewed
bombing villages and warned John F. Kennedy that "the war [will]
be won by brains and on foot." Cultural sensitivity, embedding of
staunch counterinsurgent forces (e.g., Phoenix) with local irregulars,
a systematic intelligence collection and action process, constraints
on foreign support, and the will to outlast the opposing force were
key tenets of his beliefs. In his words:

> Unless the communist subversive political organization in the
> towns and villages is broken and eliminated, the insurgent guerrilla
> units will not be defeated. If the guerrillas can be isolated from the

population, i.e. the 'little fishes' removed from 'the water', then their eventual destruction becomes automatic.

Sadly, not even at the highest levels of US diplomats or advisors was his method appreciated. Further, the not-so-subtle distinction between communist sympathizers and nationalists became blurred and gave way to America's need to apply overwhelming military might. Often lost in the fight were the aims of the rural Mekong Delta Vietnamese, the peasant or riceroots people who supplied most of that food staple consumed in Việt Nam. They wanted to farm and keep alive a hope that they may one day enjoy a peaceful and unified Việt Nam.

But the insurgent Communists had their own plan. Promoted by General Võ Nguyên Giáp, commander-in-chief of the North Vietnamese army, was the *swim with the fish* strategy. The great majority of Vietnamese people lived in the rural areas of villages and hamlets. The Việt Cộng would hide in plain sight by living among them, to appear as if a part of the population who accepted the South Việt Nam government's authority.

General Võ Nguyên Giáp
(public domain photo)

They enjoyed immunity from being exposed, partly because the government of President Nguyễn Văn Thiệu was corrupt and therefore not trusted by the common man. Also, the Việt Cộng, while operating their own indoctrination program, kept villagers in line with raids that netted funds from tax collection, and terrorized the rurals with their depredations of assassination and kidnapping. From this position, the Việt Cộng and their sympathizers could work their insurgency and proselytize their neighbors, remaining hidden, blending in, and swimming in the friendly waters with the fish.

General Giáp, a man whose abilities were not equated with his diminutive appearance at five feet tall, was one of the most prominent military strategists of modern time. His promotion of guerrilla warfare and battlefield tactics led to significant victories over both France and the United States. Giáp's methods were responsible for North Việt Nam's victories at Điện Biên Phủ in 1954 and the fall of Sài Gòn in 1975. He influenced nations around the world struggling to rid themselves of, as they saw it, colonial rule. A memorable quote attributed to the charismatic Giáp, revealing his unease with the Phoenix Program, was: "I am not concerned with the military successes of the US/GVN. I would only become concerned when the US/GVN began to destroy the Việt Cộng political infrastructure."

Gaining the trust of the peasantry—*winning their hearts and minds*—was the key for the government of South Việt Nam. The solution was political, not principally military. The Việt Cộng insurgency could not survive as a guerrilla war without rural support. But program after program, from the French to the Americans to the various governments in power in South Việt Nam, focused on the body count of enemy forces instead of working the problem from the ground up.

Perhaps unlike some American advisors in Việt Nam, I sought to take on a more subtle role of supporting the Vietnamese in their activities rather than put myself out in the commonly asserted American position of "knowing best." I was an advocate of the thinking of Trung tá (lieutenant colonel) Trần Ngọc Châu, an innovative leader of counterinsurgency methods. Châu was most recognized for his pacification efforts and the successes he enjoyed from his unique approach to winning the hearts and minds of rural Vietnamese.

He believed the war effort, particularly in counterinsurgency activity, must be taken on by the Vietnamese and not the Americans. He strongly believed Americans should operate in the background to support pacification efforts. Châu saw most Americans as having good intentions but quick to act, often with an insufficient understanding of Việt Nam and its culture.

Châu asserted the key to winning the war was to resolve the problems faced by the rural Vietnamese, troubles often instigated by the local authorities themselves. He promoted the view of the criticality of winning the trust and support of the remotest of the populace, the hamlet dwellers. He established the Static Census Grievance program, designed to convert Việt Cộng sympathizers through personal problem solving. Châu achieved remarkable success in his province of Kiến Hòa, which, like my province of service, Long An, was one of the contiguous handful referred to as the Upper Delta provinces of the Mekong Basin.

Lieutenant Colonel Châu's belief in the power of persuasion goes even further as he offered in his book *Vietnam Labyrinth: Allies, Enemies, & Why the U.S. Lost the War* (used with permission):

> If the CIA had understood the nature of the insurgency in the South in the early 1960s and succeeded in helping [coup d'état victim President] Diem counter it with appropriate policies, the war would never have escalated to the scale it reached in 1965. The bulk of the population then, 85 percent, lived in rural hamlets and villages. If more projects like my Census Grievance program and the few others that showed promise had been implemented, the [Việt Cộng] insurgency would never have become so widespread and potent.
>
> North Vietnam would have had a dilemma. Without the Việt Cộng creating both military and political problems for the South, Hồ Chí Minh's forces would have had little choice but to fight a conventional war to achieve victory. That would have been suicidal, since that was precisely the kind of war that the United States and the US-equipped and trained ARVN were prepared for—and could have won handily. Also, had the United States decided not to

overthrow Diem, American troops would not have had to venture deeply into a kind of war they did not know or understand.

Through Châu's Static Census Grievance program, Việt Cộng partisans were compromised if they chose not to accept the Census Grievance aid, forcing them to either become GVN supporters or remain as sympathizers, albeit now in a less effective position. If the SCG program was unable to persuade key Việt Cộng activists to reduce or halt their enemy activities, only as a last resort, were they targeted for neutralization through imprisonment or elimination by the military.

Although Phoenix was not strictly under the SCG program, it served as the military enforcement arm in some districts, in removing hard-core Việt Cộng who had advanced in their identity from sympathizer to political cadre. We knew these enemy men and women were part of the Việt Cộng Infrastructure, or VCI, the shadow communist civilian government that dominated large parts of rural South Việt Nam. Where my views departed from Châu's philosophy were in dealing with the Việt Cộng shadow government personalities. Although his program would eventually take military action against the VCI, the Phoenix Program's principal function was to target these men or women as enemy, allowing the rules of war to be applied.

In defining and implementing his SCG program, Lieutenant Colonel Châu made an important distinction between *two* wars, one that many US leaders failed to grasp: the *war of the generals* and their armies, modeled after US combat forces well-equipped with modern matériel; and the *real war*, as Châu put it, where the hamlet-level irregular GVN forces fought with minimal arms and equipment, and few of the enemy presented with the appearance of classic soldiers. With the local Intel Phoenix force is where I tried to make a difference. Advisors came armed with American intelligence,

The land of the peasants, the Upper Mekong Delta in Tân Trụ.

and any matériel we could scrounge for use by the poorly equipped locals who knew the neighborhoods and many of the enemy VCI personalities well. Further, Châu cautioned, seemingly peaceful areas believed to be pacified were far from being assured as free from Việt Cộng influence. He believed the government of South Việt Nam had more Việt Cộng followers than was obvious, and they were a formidable enemy capable of substantive guerrilla-style surprise attacks. This was true in the Tân Trụ district, where apparent reduced enemy activity in some hamlets was too quickly equated with military achievement and successful pacification.

While Americans in charge of the war effort denied the idea that Việt Nam was fundamentally a civil war, I encountered anecdotal evidence that tended to support it. The case of SGT Tâm comes to mind. Tâm was a Vietnamese soldier who worked in the compound operations center assisting in setting up field ops and providing targeting information. He was kept out of the field by the district chief because Tâm's brother was from North Việt Nam and was believed to be assigned to an NVA unit in our area. A wise decision from the district chief. But it also brought to me reminders of the American Civil War, often characterized as a brother-against-brother war where loyalties were split within families between the North and the South.

Corruption in South Viêt Nam was widespread, reaching into nearly every corner of governmental organizations. The Phoenix Program, as has been widely reported, was not immune. People were misrepresented as collaborators with the Viêt Cộng, based on neighborhood disputes and inter-family or political rivalries. However, district level Phoenix DIOCCs, if the district chief was not corrupt, operated effectively and successfully. In some districts, Phoenix supplied support as an assisting implementation arm of the district's Static Census Grievance tactical unit. While I supported this conceptually, in practice it was futile within Tân Trụ during my tour.

In my district of service, there were many sources already providing information about the enemy and sympathizers. They were offering "intelligence" based on supposed loyalty to the government or concern over keeping their position, not on remuneration. The quality of this information was poor to fair. Often, what we received was not actionable.

Information and its sources were rated for reliability with a widely used classification system developed during World War

The Tân Trụ DIOCC

II. As an example, the Static Census Grievance department of the government in Tân Trụ *always* rated their intelligence "C3." "C" is the source component of the rating and means the source is *fairly reliable*, having provided useful information in the past, but doubts remained about him as a source. "3" is the information reliability component and means the information is *possibly true* but remains unconfirmed. The impact to my Phoenix effort was that the moribund SCG and their information was, mostly, a waste of time. I assumed their ineffectuality, at some level, resulted from being compromised by or afraid of the Việt Cộng or wanting nothing to do with Phoenix operations. In any case, they were "F6"—reliability could not be determined—to me.

But I gleaned inferential information from their reporting. About halfway through my one-year tour, I made a temporary pin map of reports of their "C3" enemy activity and noticed that the SCG avoided reporting any information on an area three klicks from our compound. This got my attention, and I used the metadata as a basis for two subsequent operations.

I knew some areas of Tân Trụ were considered by the Việt Cộng to be travel routes or storage areas they wanted to keep secret; they needed to avoid attracting attention. The first op was for Major Ray Gravett, Tân Trụ district senior advisor, who would make one last foray into the field. I passed this target on to him, but it was unproductive. About a month later Major Gravett had rotated out, and we were going to take another run at this quiet strip of nipa palm. I got in touch with the 2/60 Recon platoon, and a CRIP operation was set up for the next morning. That evening, I was pulled out of the op to brief someone the next day from outside Tân Trụ visiting our DIOCC. Sadly, the operation made contact in the nipa quickly, showing a strong need for the enemy to defend this area. As discussed earlier, it cost the lives of two Americans from Recon.

After the CRIP returned fire and called in helicopter gunships, they pulled seventeen enemy bodies from the rubble. Multiple secondary explosions from the gunship rocket fire were seen, confirming the storage of enemy munitions. This otherwise "quiet" location appeared to be a waystation for both enemy soldiers and matériel.

Since I attended school at Fort Holabird, Maryland, and was trained as a counterintelligence agent, higher command presented me with the opportunity to employ a paid agent network of spies in Tân Trụ. The information sources of men and women were typically Vietnamese who might collect useful particulars for money from a fund I would manage as their case officer. But my opinion of the usefulness of an agent net was not positive. Several issues worked against it being successful.

My formal schooling, while exposing me to espionage tradecraft methods and techniques, did not cover them in detail. They trained me in counterintelligence, or defending against spying activities, not strictly intelligence collection. Second, I would have been practicing my craft through one or more interpreters in dealing with the Vietnamese agents. So, it was more likely that implementation of the agent handling would have occurred through Vietnamese agent handlers who would act as cutouts for me. While this approach offers some insulation between the agents and me, it would also attenuate some direct feedback I would have received from them. Finally, it could have been a significant distraction from my work of intelligence assessment directed solely at members of the Viet Cong Infrastructure.

My back-of-the-envelope analysis concluded there were too many reasons to not get involved in establishing an agent network, assuming I could do it at all. And the last thing I wished to do was to set up an agent net that might easily evolve beyond my control.

In my efforts to get close to some Vietnamese customs and culture, I got several of the Áo bà ba traditional garments, popular in the rural Mekong Delta. In particular, the so-called black pajamas pictured here were worn by the Rural Development and SCG male and female personnel as a means of identification with the riceroots peasant people.

Chapter 7
Brothers in Việt Nam

My brother George ("Chief") on the left, and I visited the USO in Vũng Tàu, Việt Nam in September 1969. His 3rd Marine Division had been pulled back from the DMZ to Okinawa and he hopped a transport to southern III Corps to visit me. I had been in country about two months and been unlucky enough to be (lightly) wounded in an ambush gone bad.

George and Bob Loewer at USO in Vũng Tàu

We took an Air America Pilatus PC-6 Porter to Vũng Tàu for a few days R&R. Air America was my required travel carrier for intracountry hops because of my job as an advisor in the covert Phoenix neutralization program.

Looking for a place to stay in Vũng Tàu, I went to the officer's club, likely the safest of places for us both. Remarkably, the compound gate guard was a red-haired Appalachian native named Jefferson with whom I had gone through basic training (I was former enlisted). It was good to see him, someone from the days of erstwhile dog-faced camaraderie between E-1 trainees.

Our names ten feet off the Vũng Tàu USO floor. I stood on Chief's shoulders to write it.

I met with the compound officer-in-charge, a first lieutenant, to get housed for a few days. But he sternly told me he would not house my brother because he was an enlisted man. He had to be an officer.

While I well understood the unusual nature of my request and the army's disdain for allowing enlisted men in the officer's club, I was somewhat miffed at that officer's choice under the circumstances. Chief was a seasoned DMZ marine, and half of a pair of brothers together in Việt Nam. There had to be exceptions.

George (Chief) Loewer writing our joint letter home.

We were headed toward the compound front gate when a junior enlisted man came running up to us and exclaimed, "The NCO In Charge wants to talk with you." I went to see him. Without fanfare, he said he would be glad to house both my brother and me. That was terrific news … and an important lesson learned by this young second lieutenant about setting things right and who to see in this man's army to get things done.

In the letter we wrote home together, while overall in a jocular tone, we stressed to those back home that worries of many folks there were not nearly as serious as those in this country. We encouraged them to put their concerns and upsets in that perspective, and to realize how comparatively good Americans had it.

The Air America Pilatus PC-6 Porter

My father once remarked of Chief to a drinking buddy, "He's more man than you and I put together." Pensive and fiercely independent, at age seventeen he rode a motorcycle west from Baltimore the length of the country and north up the Alcan highway to Anchorage, Alaska to make his own way in life. Two years later, he enlisted in the Marine Corps.

Parris Island was interesting, he told me, because he had the distinction of being the last man to be smacked by his drill instructor.

He came in country to Việt Nam as the 1969 new year ticked in. He was assigned to Fox Company, 2nd Battalion, 9th Regiment, 3rd Marine Division at Con Thien about three klicks from North Việt Nam and the DMZ. (căn cứ Cồn Tiên, meaning the "Hill of Angels"). Chief was in 1st Platoon, Fox Company, involved in Dewey Canyon in the A Shau (A Sầu) valley.

I received a letter from Chief, written on March 7, 1969. He had finished an operation and returned to LZ Stud, also known as FSB Vandegrift, when his unit was advised they would go out again, this time to Khe Sanh. They had to wait out a persistent fog blanket, spending the time in full gear until their choppers could take off. But he did not object too much to the Khe Sanh duty of "standing lines" because, unlike some field operations, they had regular c-rations and water available.

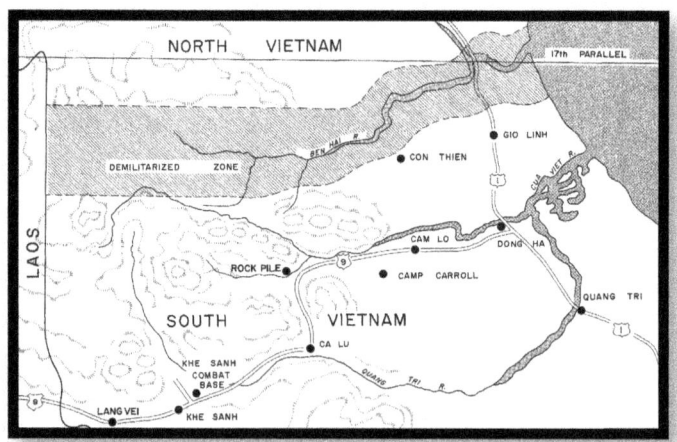

Cồn Tiên and its proximity to the DMZ (public domain image)

The duration of the Khe Sanh duty was indeterminate. They were waiting for Golf Company of 2/9 to return from the bush to join them for two or three days of R & R. Golf was busy holding the perimeter around Erskin Support Base (Hill 406) while it was dismantled and choppered out. Chief noted that while he was there,

Hill 406 was probed and attacked one morning at daybreak. Their R & R was scheduled to be at Cua Viet (Cửa Việt), a secured area on the coast with opportunities for swimming and sunning. Something well-earned and worth looking forward to.

Like many of us who put in our time in Việt Nam, Chief grew and groomed a mustache. My view is we, as those chosen to kill for our elected representatives, wanted a different persona when in the field. We were, in Việt Nam, necessarily a different person. And for some of us when leaving Việt Nam, we would right ourselves and resume our true identities by shaving it off. Retrospectively, it was right-headed thinking but so naïve when believing it could help as a psychological remedy for us, notwithstanding our determination.

Photos courtesy G. Loewer

One afternoon when we were both back in the World, Chief related how he used earwax to stabilize and curl the handlebars on his mustache. He went on to tell me about the time when he was sleeping, one of his platoon members cut off half of his mustache as a joke. While he found some humor in it as he recounted the event, it had to have made him angry. It would have had it been me.

By the time I returned from Việt Nam back to the World, Chief had finished his term of service and his biggest worry was the scars from jungle rot he had sustained. His condition was not helped by the VA, who refused him medical care despite his obvious Việt Nam-related injury. These were the days of Richard Nixon and his order to the VA to "go slow" in aiding veterans, even those injured in combat.

I believe Chief's rank was lance corporal, but I am uncertain. I know that he, not unlike me, had a disdain for some formalities of rank. He was quite comfortable showing that attitude in the bush by not answering to any name but the childhood moniker "Chief."

George "Chief" Loewer, on the far right, near Con Thien.
Photo courtesy G. Loewer

For those who are genuinely involved in war fighting, it is more common than not to have experienced one or more events whose memories cannot be escaped no matter the time that has passed. Such was the case of Clarke, a platoon mate of Chief's.

On a patrol near the DMZ, Chief's unit came upon a river and paralleled it when suddenly activity appeared on the opposing bank. They paused their movement and hunkered down, waiting to assess what was happening across the river. They soon realized it was NVA regulars moving through the area. Although the squad leader directed everyone to keep quiet and let the enemy patrol pass by, weapon fire began and was returned by the NVA. In the process, Private Clarke sustained a wound from which he later died. When the enemy encounter was reported in detail back at base camp, the patrol leader was written up for cowardice for refusing to follow the rules of engagement with the enemy. Undeservedly, Chief took on the sting of Clarke's death, feeling a sense of responsibility and brotherhood. When back in the World, he drove from his home in Baltimore to the deep South to visit Clarke's family and provided a first-hand account of what had happened to their son.

While I never discussed Chief's feelings of survivor guilt with him, I knew, like my own, it was a powerful sense of *there must have been another way.*

Photos courtesy G. Loewer

Chapter 8

In and Around the
Advisor's Hooch

A baking aroma in the hooch after lunch was a strong indicator I was doing my cake thing for the team. We all tried to contribute to our wartime home in ways that pulled us together as group members. And it was easy to whip out a cake. The baking mixture was canned for the military. Add two eggs, some water/milk, preheat oven to 350, bake for thirty-five minutes, and voilà.

Bà Bà, our Vietnamese house woman, thought my occasional culinary contribution amusing. She was a ruggedly handsome woman, late thirties, with a cheerful, upbeat disposition. She enjoyed being around Americans, making her an exceptionally suitable match for the team. It was not difficult to recognize the curvy figure under her áo bà ba (pajamas). More than one man in our group would tease her about how attractive she was. For men without women, she was compelling but unavailable as she would readily indicate to a particular staff sergeant: "You no have mama san; you horny. Me have papa san; me no horny."

Bà Bà cooked our breakfast and dinner. Along with the younger Cô Cháu, they kept the household running and tidy. Lunchtime for me was my food favorite, repeated over and over. Hey, I knew what I liked. Canned beans mixed with scrounged hamburger meat did the trick. Easy clean up, too. The beans came in a single-serving can, sixty cans to a case.

Much of the matériel we used and food we consumed was scrounged from US military units within a day's jeep ride. This included munitions, some of which we would give to the Vietnamese. It was nationally a commonplace occurrence but thankfully rarely in Tân Trụ, that the Vietnamese would ask for stuff—"Thiếu úy, you souvenir me from the PX?" Most of "our" Vietnamese understood Americans did not appreciate requests like this. During my entire tour, I heard it only twice.

My training at Engineer OCS paid dividends from time-to-time. I had asked for and been given a case of C4 plastic explosive, blasting caps, fuse, and fuse igniters from the US battalion commander at the nearby 2/60. He was open to passing us supplies because we helped the US interface with the Vietnamese, and I gave him actionable intelligence. To be sure, it was not a case of my intelligence always being accurate. But the point was it was more accurate than that of his S-2 intelligence officer, Captain Greg Barker.

One of the difficult-to-obtain munitions was MK3 concussion grenades. These were important to me because standard M26A1 grenades were ordnance that peppered the enemy with shrapnel and often killed the targets when thrown into the bunker they occupied.

In the world of Phoenix, we sought to capture the enemy instead of kill. The old maxim of *dead men tell no tales* is well understood in the intelligence community. A captured enemy might give useful information; a dead one could not. Thus the preference for concussion grenades over the traditional fragmentation type. But they were difficult to scrounge.

So, I made them. My hand-crafted concussion grenades packed a tremendous wallop. I bent half of a C4 block over on itself, using the adhesive surface to mold it into a chunkier mass. Pushing through the C4 plastic wrapper with the handle of a crimping tool, I created a hole that would accommodate a blasting cap. When ignited, blasting caps sent out a shock wave that detonated other substances; in this case, the C4 plastic explosive. When going on a mission, I would ensure we carried the C4 and blasting caps on separate choppers, about all I could do for safety concerns.

Looking back on this bit of innovation, I must laugh at my lack of concern about the explosives. Much to the chagrin of SFC Crowe who bunked nearby in our hooch, I kept the case of C4 blocks under my cot. It seemed a reasonable thing to do, although an on-target incoming rocket or mortar that penetrated the PSP (pierced steel plank) in the ceiling could explode the C4, giving the Việt Cộng a terribly satisfying result.

Under the heading of regrettable actions, I must place my written response to a young woman who wrote a letter "to any Vietnam soldier." Higher command passed these out to us on the absolute condition we not fail to respond to them.

The energetic young woman who wrote the letter I was handed clearly liked men in the military, particularly men whose lives were at risk in a war zone. Her letter was in fact initially remarkably effective. Hearing such laudatory remarks from a woman my age about my contribution, someone she did not know detail on at all, was both uplifting and heartwarming. As I continued to read, I thought how worthwhile this letter-writing program was and how much I appreciated having the overall rightness of what I was doing confirmed by someone whose opinion mattered to me. Men at war are open to confirmation that our work was appreciated. We particularly cared what our nation's women thought of us performing our duty.

As I reached the end of the letter, she summed it all up by saying, "I dig you guys over there, I just don't dig what you are doing." That remark struck me like a slap in the face. I believe now that she meant no harm in saying that, probably intending to convey her disgust for war. But it sadly was not received that way.

I was obligated to respond, and so I did. While I was civil as I wrote back to her, I left no doubt how I felt about her concluding remark. Perhaps a better man would have overlooked her statement. But she left me with a sense of contributing to a war atrocity recently in the news. I did not like that feeling. That was not who we were and not what we did. Had her letter come toward the end of my tour when I had greater perspective and maturity, I probably would have responded differently.

Wartime accidents are a genuine tragedy, and they occur with surprising frequency. By some estimates, fully one-quarter of casualties in war result from friendly fire accidents. On a break from the monsoon rain mid-morning in June 1970, one of our team members was admiring and cleaning his revolver. As stories like this go, the weapon accidentally discharged, ricocheted, and struck downward through the lower jaw of our dog, Slick. The bullet entered through his open mouth under his tongue and exited out his jaw. Slick howled in pain, but that was short-lived. Over the next few days, he recovered from the wound and soon was his old self again.

In one sense, Slick was incredibly lucky. The penetration of his lower jaw hit no bone, teeth, tongue, or anything but soft tissue. The shooter, careless in his activity, was beside himself with cries

Slick, hurrying me back to the compound at the conclusion of an operation

of an anguished "I shot Slick!" But shit happens, adjustments are made, and we try harder.

I recall an incident that could have cost the lives of more than a few Vietnamese soldiers. I was in the Tân Trụ radio room one afternoon when a wide-eyed Vietnamese TOC man came running in and shouting that a Máy Bay (helicopter) was shooting rockets at his troops. He thrust his finger on a map grid square and I grabbed the horn. "Tanker, Tanker 262!" "Tanker, Tanker 262!" I shouted. "262, this is Tanker" came the province TOC reply. I exclaimed, "You've got somebody dropping shit on my people! Grid XS684652!" While the province TOC radioman asked me to stand by so he could investigate, the attacking helicopter pilot, already tuned in to our *push*, heard my transmission and saw that he was the offending chopper. He stopped his bombing run at once and radioed to me what had happened. No one hurt. *Phew! Too close for comfort*, I thought. These kinds of errors happen when coordination between disparate friendly force units is poorly executed. Fortunately, in Tân Trụ they were rare and caused nothing but a bit of excitement.

There was a phenomenon in Viêt Nam among advisors and their counterparts known as the *friendly ambush*. The Vietnamese were masters at knowing when to ask for something, usually ordnance or perhaps something from the PX. Alternatively, the ambush could be associated with a social activity such as having a drink. This was one they liked to pull on newly assigned advisors.

The local rice wine had a high alcohol content and was quite popular among rural Vietnamese. Our counterparts seemed to take a special delight in coercing and watching young advisors, many of whom were not regular drinkers, to down a shot of the clear liquid, then gasp for breath after being surprised at the potency of this often 40% ABV drink.

Since advisors were de facto representatives of our country, we worked to make nice. We did not put our hands on our hips or cross our arms often; that was considered culturally rude. We did not pat kids on the top of their heads; that was condescending and disrespectful. But we did drink sometimes when "invited" to. Hence, the friendly ambush. And we accepted our male counterpart's preference for holding hands while walking, as was commonplace among Vietnamese men who were good friends.

Improvements in economic, medical, and social conditions in outlying areas of Viêt Nam were sought through the Rural Development Cadre program, an initiative focusing on encouraging enhancement of the quality of life and self-defense. Some advisors worked directly with the RD Vietnamese. Our contribution was to lend a hand when we were not busy with wartime activities.

As this photograph shows, imagination and practicality can go a long way toward satisfying those goals. Here from left to right are Captain Bob Wooten, SGT "L", and SFC Crowe. They scrounged a piece of four-by-eight plywood and are covering it with flat black paint. The resulting blackboard was used in the local one-room schoolhouse for the children.

One of the MAT team advisors, First Lieutenant Nelson Brashears, integrated with the Vietnamese at a level many of us could only aspire to. A former Peace Corps member, Nelson understood very well the life of the riceroots people, the hamlet and village dwellers, and sought to identify with them. Here is Nelson with some of his Vietnamese friends, and in his military garb, giving a tactical briefing to his father. Nelson's dad visited our district from his job with Pacific Architects and Engineers, an American defense and government services contractor working in Viêt Nam.

Not exactly rural development but helpful nonetheless was our resupply mission. Sometimes it involved us procuring the supplies, sometimes facilitating their transport. Here we see SFC Mosley on the right signaling the helicopter to move upward with the load and depart while an unnamed Vietnamese is holding his hat to avoid its loss from the rotor wash. Mosley was a country boy, unassuming and pleasant to work with, and along with

SFC Charles Jones from Seat Pleasant, Maryland on the left, invaluable to this young lieutenant in learning his job.

While we had some comforts of home in our hooch, fine art wall hangings were not one of them. Absent Playmate pictorials, something appropriate to break up the monotony of the gray-green walls became necessary. After all, this was not a barracks and our cots sat out in the open in each cramped, doorless adjoining room. I found that snipping magazine photos of other kinds of natural subjects more than acceptable. This collage above my cot distracted from the day's events as I lay there waiting for sleep to overtake my thoughts of what the day had brought.

There was the occasional macabre activity. Not the stick-in-your-mind unpleasantness like enemy bodies lying alongside Thunder Road, although that happened intermittently. And not the carrying of one end of a friendly soldier's body off a helicopter, his head hanging low from lax neck muscles, which also happened. But actions taken by personnel, often American, to replace fear and discomfort with putative humor. This skull, I was told, was found after a heavy rain during the monsoon season. One of the MAT team NCOs thought it a hoot to mount it on their team's jeep. NCOs had no corner on this type of activity. We could see officers participating as well. In war, this kind of comic relief and pressure release happens.

When there were enough team members up for it, we would gather around the dining table at dusk for a few hands of rummy. Invariably, we would hear one or more hand grenade explosions as some less competent Vietnamese Regional Forces would accidentally walk into their own trip-wired ambushes. To be fair to them, ambush discipline is more difficult in the dark, particularly when the number of troops involved increases. These RF units often put a sizeable part of their companies into the nighttime operations.

SFC DeYoung, a MAT team member, standing in front of the advisor's hooch.

Guess who came to dinner? Truth-be-told, it was after dinner during one of our evening card-playing games. Suddenly, a lightning-quick snake came slithering from the woodwork next to our hooch bunker, and we could not get on the table fast enough. We trapped him and took him outside. He appeared to be a viper, so he was killed. The

An unidentified but venomous appearing snake, KIA

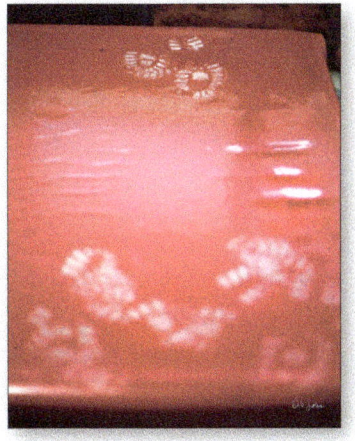

Footprints on the tabletop from a soldier who prefers anonymity

appearance of an apparently venomous snake in our hooch was at the least unsettling. We had captured documents that contained details—about some US advisors resident in the compound by rank, and which of the buildings housed them. Further, the documents implied Việt Cộng spies had either visited or were residents of the compound. It was generally known that the Việt Cộng had put a price on the head on Phoenix personnel, particularly US military or civilian. It was not a stretch of the imagination to consider whether this possibly venomous snake had help getting into our hooch.

Every once in a while, just for grins, we would play with vintage weapons, out of service and discarded. One of the MAT teams came across a belt fed MK18 40 mm grenade launcher. It was old and hand-crank driven. On this occasion, we had lots of 40 mm HE ammunition, so this kids game became instantly clear. Could a person turn the crank fast enough to put an entire belt through the launcher before the first round hit the ground? Well, no was the answer. The armament had been discarded, probably by the Navy, likely deployed on former model US river patrol boats. It was not usable by ground troops, but we found it an engaging diversion.

While drug use by US troops in Việt Nam is well documented, it was not part of the life of Advisory Team 86 in Tân Trụ during my tour. Perhaps that statement speaks more to the social circles I frequented. There was one occasion when I encountered illegal drugs, and it was nearly a non-event. I was returning on foot to our compound from a visit to the 2/60 two klicks away, when a middle-aged woman approached me holding a shopping bag-sized clear plastic sack of dried marijuana leaves. She spoke only Vietnamese, offering to sell some to me. In those days, I was a Dudley Do-Right sort. I did not like drug use, particularly in a war zone. Indeed, it was not until the age of thirty-five before I tried pot.

Chapter 9
Slick

Meet *Slick*. He came to us from the US 101st Airborne Division, famous for their air assault capability. Slick occasionally went on ops with us until he jumped out of an insertion chopper early, mistakenly thinking the top of the tall rice plants was the ground. We retired him after that. He was appearing rather distinguished anyway, gray muzzle and all.

We took amusement to break the tension and sometimes horror of the job when and wherever we could. We had a serious rat problem, but then, who did not? Nonetheless, having them crawl over us when trying to get a night's sleep had to stop.

There were two types of rats in our compound, the smelly and the not so smelly. We had to minimize their presence, so we used cages to *trap* them. (Hey, we were advisors, not front-line troops.) Using the best bait available—black crow candy from Sundry packs—we set the traps at night. Sundry packs were boxes of personal items issued to troops, which included candy that no one else wanted. By morning we usually had a few odorous prisoners before the Vietnamese honor guard saluted the sunrise and raised their country's flag up the compound flagpole.

As their daily reveille ceremony began, we would call our dog Slick to the ready. We would release the rats in the compound, to Slick's delight. He would chase and kill whatever he could, distracting the at-attention Vietnamese troops from the flag-raising ritual. Slick's kill record was about one in three. Two of the rats lived to fight another day. And the ever-patient Vietnamese once again tolerated their crazy American counterparts' behavior.

I must admit, Slick's exploits went beyond the district compound rat chasing. He charged into at least one bunker after a Việt Cộng,

SSG Jay McAlister cradling Slick's puppies

but frankly, his lack of adroitness was showing his age even then. And he must have picked up on us soft balling his tasking. Slick adopted a more relaxed lifestyle and made time to find a dog of the female persuasion he liked. The outcome of that operation is in the picture. SSG McAlister sits with two of Slick's puppies. Slick—what a guy!

PART TWO

The Best of Times,
the Worst of Times

Chapter 10
The Choppers, Our Lifeline

Over the fifteen years of the Viêt Nam experience, more than 12,000 helicopters were deployed in the *helicopter war*. About 5,000 of them were lost to hostile action or accidents. Nearly 5,000 pilots and crew of the 40,000 who served lost their lives.

The heroism of the air crews saved countless lives and to the men like me who operated on the ground in one capacity or another fell a debt we could never fully repay. In my experience of calling for and directing gunships, they were always up for whatever we asked, no

matter the risk. Dustoffs, or medical evacuation helicopters, would pick up wounded men in virtually all combat conditions.

In our area of operation, Tân Trụ district, we benefited from the skills of Greyhounds and Mad Dogs with the 240th Assault Helicopter Company, Spartans from the 190th AHC, and others. Here is

a Mad Dog calling card, one of a couple I have that M. H. Forrester tossed out to us on the ground. I interpret them as a combination of pride in mission accomplishment and perhaps daring fate.

Early in my tour, I had an unforgettable helicopter visual reconnaissance (VR) in a Hughes OH-6 Cayuse loach, not unlike that in the photo. When I first buckled into the loach, the pilot asked how high I wanted to do the reconnaissance. I wrote on the area map he held out to me, "500 feet." He took the grease pencil from my hand and wrote a "1" in front of the "500," then wrote "or 50" beneath. I smiled and pointed to fifty feet.

The pilot was a true wizard, flying rolled over ninety degrees on our side to effect enemy-evading sharp high-speed turns above the

Hughes OH-6 Cayuse loach

mangroved enemy territory, including segments of the Vàm Cỏ Đông river. He quick-turned it left and right for about fifteen minutes until the *engine chip* light appeared on the cockpit instrument panel. He sat us down immediately, choosing a small clearing in this remote area known as the elbow—the middle of nowhere in Việt Cộng country. After the rough, hurried landing and a lightning-fast engine and gear checkout, he felt comfortable enough to take to the air. We headed back to our compound and did not encounter resistance along the way. It was a high pucker factor, but safe ending.

> Engine chip—Engine chip detectors can sense metal chips in engine or transmission oil. In a combat zone, this can indicate the aircraft may have taken enemy fire with damage to its engine or components. It is considered an emergency, and the recommended action is to land the helicopter at once.

About a month after my tour began, my predecessor had rotated out when I learned a firefly mission was scheduled for me. Firefly operations were army aviation nighttime warfare search and destroy missions carried out in our area by two helicopters acting together, employing unique flight tactics. The first was the search chopper that held command personnel and housed a large searchlight, shining it on the ground looking for enemy targets. Often, this chopper would nose over the nipa palm below 200 feet in altitude, making themselves an exceedingly easy target. The second helicopter was a gunship that attacked anything of interest the search chopper would find or provoke.

This was my second firefly mission since arriving in country, and the first I was to supervise as the observer in the C&C aircraft. Firefly excursions were a tool available to me if I found them useful. My first firefly mission had been extraordinarily difficult. In the pitch-black night, the C&C helicopter would fly in small circles, lighting the terrain, searching for enemy activity. The gunship would perform attack runs underneath our flight path, destroying whatever we had our searchlight on. The exploding ordnance brought a hell of a light show, and for me, it was extremely disorienting. Since my childhood days, vertigo had been a rare but persistent problem. At amusement parks, I could not tolerate rides that moved me in circles. I would become disoriented and sometimes nauseated. This circling search chopper "ride," necessary to discourage enemy weapons fire, proved to be no different.

The chopper arrived for the firefly mission, so I showed up and strapped into the seat adjacent to the Huey door gunner. Truth be told, I was apprehensive of possible enemy contact from the last op that had been so disastrous, killing seven of our number. We had not gone far at all when the vertigo symptoms manifested, like the last firefly mission, giving me a strong sense of unsettlement and an inability to judge orientation. My body's vestibular system seemed to not be working correctly, and I had no sense of proper spatial orientation. Years later I realized I had a propensity for this problem to appear.

But this night, with the chopper making its way with movement on all three axes, I was at a major disadvantage. The disorientation and my lack of "sea legs" rendered me inert and hesitant. It interfered with my communicating with the pilot so much that the operation had to be called off. For me, it was a case of extreme embarrassment at failing to perform the mission and wasting the valuable helicopter blade hours in an unproductive outing.

I made a vow that night—I would not again allow myself to be in that circumstance as part of a firefly mission. The combination of nighttime inky blackness, the chopper making small circle revolutions over enemy territory, watching the successive ground objects lit up by our searchlight while circling, and my compromised vestibular system all came together to bring this op to a screeching halt. That was the end of firefly missions for me. I had more productive things to do.

In the late 1960s, the draft was going strong. A lot of men were pulled into the Việt Nam War, some rough-and-tumble characters, others perhaps more introspective, less into fisticuffs. For both Americans and Vietnamese, this was the way of it.

We were on a daylight Phoenix mission going after a member of the VCI—the Việt Cộng Infrastructure—the enemy's hidden civilian government that was highly active in South Việt Nam. As we walked into the target village, a Việt Cộng moved into the open, running away from us. We followed him to a nearby stream that was perhaps twenty feet wide and at least eight feet deep. We saw two footprints on the mud bank, widely spaced apart, that led to the water—a clear sign he had run into the stream. But he was nowhere to be seen.

We needed a broader perspective to ensure this guy had not moved further up or downstream, so we radioed to see if a Loach

The ink-stained communism flag we captured

hunter helicopter was available to assist. The broadcast "VC on the run" got a quick response and within a few minutes we had a Loach moving slowly over the nipa palm on the riverbank searching for our guy. It was not long before the Loach found him, spraying him with M134 six-barrel 7.62 mm minigun fire as the Việt Cộng tried escaping across a nearby rice paddy.

Things looked routine as we approached the form on the ground. The surprise was what we found when we searched the body. In addition to the bright red hammer-and-sickle flag, we found one-inch rubber squares cut from flip-flops, labeled with what appeared to be Chinese writing differentiating the pieces. These were pieces of a game, likely *Cờ tướng* (*Capture the King*).

Cờ tướng game pieces with its original packaging

But we took a pause when we opened a hand-sized booklet he had closed over four stubby colored pencils. The Việt Cộng's colored-pencil artwork was of some of the most beautiful drawings of flowers in that medium I had seen.

We had done our job well and killed the enemy according to our rules of engagement. But we had also, by the evidence in front of us, killed a gentle, thoughtful man who, like some others, probably did not belong in a war zone. Certainly, this man was not an innocent bystander. But at this time, in this place, war was a somewhat different story. Even to the most battle-hardened warriors among us, action of this nature left cracks in the masks of ferocity we applied to protect our vulnerable sides.

Lieutenant Colonel Jim McDaniel served two tours in Việt Nam as a slick and gunship pilot. In his second tour in I Corps, he supported the Army of the Republic of Việt Nam (ARVN). The Vietnamese people were taking greater responsibility for the war effort, while America was gradually withdrawing its troops.

Jim's call sign, Hornet 20, uniquely identified him as part of the 116th Assault Helicopter Company operating to support the Americal Division at Chu Lai, roughly ninety klicks south of Đà Nẵng in I Corps. Jim finished his second tour before Christmas of 1971 with 1,700 total combat flight hours in Việt Nam, the basic load of forty-four Air Medals, a Purple Heart, Bronze Star, and others. He relates one of the many stories from his tours flying both Huey slicks and gunships for Americal, assisting the soldiers of Việt Nam in holding onto their country.

In July 1971, I was a captain on my second tour flying helicopters in Việt Nam and was my unit's "Standardization Instructor Pilot", the senior instructor pilot in the unit. I was flying in the left seat as aircraft commander and flight lead of a formation of seven UH-1H Huey helicopters. We were on a combat extraction in the mountains fifteen to twenty klicks southwest of Trà Bồng, a village southwest of Chu Lai, the Americal Division headquarters on the banks of the Trà Bồng River. The village is at the western edge of the coastal plains in the foothills of the mountains. We were extracting

Vietnamese ARVN soldiers after we had inserted them during a combat assault into a different landing zone (LZ) the day before.

As the US, at that time, was in the beginning stages of preparation for withdrawal from Viêt Nam, more and more of the combat operations were being conducted by ARVN soldiers rather than Americans. This ARVN unit was acting as a "Quick Reaction Force," not unlike Vietnamese in the Phoenix Program, that could be rapidly deployed to support another unit in contact or where intelligence reports indicated the likelihood of North Vietnamese Army regulars or Viêt Cộng activity.

The mountains form quickly from the plains in this region, and it was mountainous where we were to extract the troops. They had been inserted by us the day before in an LZ further up in the mountains and they had made a sweep down a valley looking for a reported NVA unit along a known infiltration route of the Hồ Chí Minh trail. We were to pick up the ARVNs that afternoon and return them to their base camp at Trà Bồng.

CPT James McDaniel. Photo courtesy of Jim McDaniel.

The approach and landing to the pickup zone (PZ) were uneventful. No enemy fire was reported or received. Because the friendly Vietnamese troops had swept the valley area and had cleared the PZ, our approach was cold—our door gunners did not fire their M-60 machine guns for suppressive fire.

The PZ was a long, narrow clear area in the bottom of the valley and was just large enough to accommodate all the helicopters of the flight in trail, one behind the other. I had the flight form a trail formation on final approach and we all landed in the PZ. Again, I was the lead aircraft, and I was at the flight controls.

Six ARVN soldiers with field gear and weapons got on our helicopter. After receiving an "up" from the trail helicopter (meaning all aircraft were loaded), I lifted off and began a climb out and up the valley directly in front of me, in the direction from which the Vietnamese soldiers had swept. This meant gaining relative altitude between the helicopter and the treetops was slow because the terrain was rising as I climbed out. This is not normally the optimal flight path to take, as it is generally best to get altitude as quickly as possible. However, I chose this departure path for two reasons. First, the Vietnamese had cleared the area, and to depart down the valley, the direction from which we had arrived, I would have had to make a sharp turn toward the other aircraft behind me.

Shortly after I began overflying the trees at the far end of the clearing, we took heavy small arms and automatic weapons fire from nearly directly below and to the sides of the helicopter. Our altitude was still quite low as the terrain was rising in our direction of flight. I would approximate our altitude at less than 100 feet over the treetops. The NVA had apparently followed the ARVNs down the mountainside and, knowing they were going to be picked up by helicopters, were waiting for us to appear.

We took multiple hits in the aircraft and my copilot, Warrant Officer William Moorewood, was hit in the leg. Moorewood was

Taken after the chin bubble had been washed down and cleaned up. Note the co-pilot's seat is still laying back on the cargo floor. Photo courtesy of Jim McDaniel.

a new pilot in the unit, on his first combat assault mission in Viêt Nam, and I was giving him his initial operational mission checkout. He took a bullet through the helicopter chin bubble and it impacted his left leg above the top of his boot, traveling up his calf muscle toward his knee. Another shot entered through the windshield, missing me by inches. I felt the impact of several other hits to the helicopter. In addition to Moorewood, the door gunner on the right side of the helicopter, and one of the ARVN soldiers were also hit.

When the copilot was shot, his reflective reaction caused his left leg to hit the cyclic control, used to move the helicopter to the side, forward, or backward. At the same time, his right foot jerked, kicking the tail rotor foot pedal. The force almost knocked the cyclic control out of my hand, and the right pedal input induced an extreme yawing of the helicopter. Our airspeed was still low, perhaps only thirty knots, and we were in immediate danger of hitting the treetops as the helicopter entered an uncontrolled steep turn. If I could not bring it under control at once, we would hit the trees within seconds. As I struggled with the controls, I also simultaneously keyed the microphone switch on the cyclic control and radioed to the rest of the flight that I was taking hits and not to follow my flight path—to break either right or left. They did so and no other helicopter took hits.

As I was trying to control the aircraft, Moorewood was yelling and grabbing for his leg. He kept hitting the flight controls with his hands and legs, making it exceedingly difficult to bring the helicopter back under control. After having initially returned fire with his M-60 machine gun, within seconds of recognizing that the copilot was hit and I was having trouble controlling the aircraft, my crew chief Specialist Mathew Arnaudo had unstrapped, jumped forward, and had released the locking device on the copilot's seat and rotated him rearward into the cargo area and away from the flight controls. The two pilots' armored seats had a release handle on the back for the two front legs of the seat and a

Two exit holes in the roof from bullets that entered the cockpit and narrowly missed Captain McDaniel in the left pilot's seat. Photo courtesy Jim McDaniel.

Four helicopters of the seven-ship formation en route to the pickup zone. Note the mountainous terrain. Photo courtesy of Jim McDaniel.

swivel connection on the rear two legs. Pulling the release handle unlocked the front legs and allowed the seat to be rotated back on the rear legs so it could lay flat in the cargo section. This action allowed a wounded pilot to be removed from the seat without interfering with any flight controls, likely saving all our lives as it allowed me to regain control of the helicopter and avoid impact with the trees.

This was a rather tense moment for both of us. From my standpoint, I did not know how badly the helicopter had been shot up, or even whether it would continue to fly. We had taken multiple rounds through the cockpit and cargo areas. I was actively looking for a place large enough to autorotate the helicopter into should the engine quit. The problem was the rugged mountains. There were no suitable landing areas, and where we would have to go was also where the NVA were located.

The old girl continued to fly. However, given we had a lot of bullet holes in the aircraft and I had no idea where most of them went or what they went through, my focus centered on the engine, its rotor RPMs, and the system's temperatures and pressures. Amazingly, they all remained in the "green," suggesting the Huey would probably keep on flying. As I continued my climb out and flight back to Chu Lai, Specialist Arnaudo applied first aid to control Moorewood's badly bleeding leg wound while he was lying on his back, still strapped into his seat. He also attended to the wounds of the ARVN soldier and the door gunner who had taken a round in his buttocks that travelled upward into his body cavity. I proceeded directly to and landed at the Division's 90th Evacuation Hospital helipad in Chu Lai where the doctors took both crew members directly into surgery. Both the copilot and the gunner were wounded seriously enough to be medevac'd out of Viêt Nam and back to the States for extended treatment and recovery.

CPT James McDaniel relaxing while waiting on the signal to crank while shutdown in the field on a quick reaction standby. Photo courtesy of Jim McDaniel.

Arnaudo later told me that he could not get Moorewood's seat all the way down to the floor when he released his seat to get him away from the flight controls. When we landed at the hospital pad and the Medics removed Moorewood from his seat, an ARVN soldier crawled out from under the seat back. During the entire return flight, perhaps half-an-hour, that ARVN soldier was trapped under the heavily armored seat.

By his immediate covering fire and the lightning speed in which Specialist Arnaudo analyzed the seriousness of the situation and responded by removing the copilot from interfering with the controls, he very probably saved us from crashing into the trees. He also likely saved the lives of either or both the copilot and the door gunner by rendering immediate first aid and controlling their bleeding.

I submitted Specialist Arnaudo for the Distinguished Flying Cross for his actions that day.

Jim McDaniel

Our Greyhound friends lifted supplies from our district compound to a remote outpost five klicks away. The American in the photo is SFC Mosley assigned as a member of Advisory Team 86 in Tân Trụ. He is hooking up a sling of matériel under this Huey to be carried to the remote outpost pictured below. The outpost was in an isolated hamlet a klick south from the "elbow" of Tân Trụ, a staging area for Việt Cộng/NVA forces during Tet of 1968. The many craters there evidenced the heavy bombing it received.

Note the chain link fencing behind the moat. It stopped about forty percent of B40/41s rocket propelled grenades (RPGs) fired at the

compound. One function we advisors had was to scrounge matériel and supplies for the Vietnamese such as this vital outpost fencing. As inferred from the outpost photos, the area was under Việt Cộng control during the night, like much of Tân Trụ in 1969.

There was one occasion in the spring of 1970 when a UH-1H Huey helicopter, not apparently outfitted for battle, was flying overhead. The pilot must have been bored on their flight and, seeing a lone vehicle on this remote dirt road, made a tight circle around our jeep from about three hundred feet altitude. I was on Thunder Road, the unpaved artery from the province capital to our district compound, driving my M151 jeep to Tân An to pick up the team's mail. SP4 Mendez, an RTO and more recent addition to the team, was riding shotgun.

As our jeep bounced along over this unimproved road, the chopper made a swooping dive toward us as if he were executing a rocket attack run. Giving up half a smile of recognition, I thought *this is different*. His continuation of this activity twice more, though, dispelled any view I might have of shrugging this off as an acceptable lark.

The Việt Cộng knew only too well there are few sensations of alarm that equal that of a chopper making a direct firing pattern run at you in apparent preparation for letting go a salvo of 70 mm Mighty Mouse rockets. Well, this was far from my first rodeo. I had been on the ground many times when the gunships made their attack passes as we requested.

As the hotdogging pilot continued to play his game of making rocket runs at us, I had enough and instructed my RTO to brandish his M16 at the ready, in clear view of the chopper crew. The tactic worked. The chopper pilot broke off his attack game, and we continued our drive to get the mail. That was the only time I can remember feeling less than enthused about helicopters and their crews.

On another occasion when we called in gunships for close air support to pound an enemy position, CPT Bob Wooten, deputy district senior advisor and I were too close when the helicopter fired his rockets. We quickly had to hit the ground and turn our backs to the explosions. It was our mistake and a unique experience, almost like being on the receiving end. Our proximity to the munitions going off was such that we could feel pieces of the rocket casing hitting our backs. As the gunship was circling to line up for his next run, we quickly searched through the vegetation and found what had stung our backs yet did not pierce our fatigues. We grabbed what appeared to be pieces of plastic O-ring girdles from the rockets, something I was not able to verify with someone who might know more about these munitions. Then we *đi đi mau*'d to a more comfortable distance.

Infrequently, I would have the option of using more exotic helicopter assets such as "people sniffers." These were devices designed to detect from altitude the substance ammonia, a lighter-than-air compound and component of sweat and urine. This equipment was UH-1 Huey-mounted and known as the M-3 personnel detector. While it was regarded as overly sensitive, it could detect troops firing weapons even when well hidden.

My onetime use of the M-3 on a Huey chopper was not fruitful. The pilot complained during much of the mission of the exceedingly sensitive equipment that yielded poor results. However, other organizations in the Delta apparently had better results than we did, as has been reported in the literature.

We had been inserted near An Nhựt Tân village in a sweep operation a few klicks east of Tân An, the provincial capital of Long An. It was an area not typically associated with ongoing enemy activity, but it was near the supply line originating at the large enemy matériel depot in Ba Tu, Cambodia known as the Parrot's Beak. The Ba Tu encampment was rumored to support weapons manufacturing facilities, and American prisoners had reportedly been held there.

A troop insertion in Tân Trụ about to take place

Vietnamese troops and I were first put down on the north side of the waterway with intelligence reports indicating Việt Cộng guerrillas in the area. It was a hot LZ, so door gunners on both sides of the choppers fired continuously, both going in and lifting out. A good move, but when inserting on the opposite side of the river a few minutes later, the gunners repeated the same activity that caused M60 machine gun fire from north-facing gunners to rain down on us as they fired when lifting out.

I grabbed the horn and told the Command and Control chopper to stop the door gunner fire. It stopped. No one hit, all well and good, but then the Command and Control captain, doing the talking for the colonel, dismissed me with "I will *caution* the door gunner."

After being shot up and diving behind patty dikes into mud, his genteel language hit a nerve.

I took the handset and unartfully yelled, "You tell that fucking door gunner…" All the captain could say after a stunned pause was, "Watch your language." Two weeks later I was at the MACV compound in Tân An, the provincial capital, to pick up the team's mail, and the enlisted guys were still laughing about my profane radio communication.

Apparently, due to the operation's proximity to Tân An city, my entire cursing session was loud and clear in the province Tactical Operations Center (TOC). And I have to say, it reinforced my feelings of being closer to enlisted guys than officers. "You're Lieutenant Loewer, right? We heard you on the radio." There were smiles all around. I was formerly enlisted, and I appreciated the humor.

Chapter 11
The Death of Hồ Chí Minh

Hồ Chí Minh, president and longtime revolutionary leader of North Việt Nam, died on September 2, 1969. He was revered by the local Việt Cộng and his death, even by heart failure, was expected to provoke a reaction against the government of South Việt Nam.

An intelligence report from the Vietnamese National Police office—close to our compound—indicated sometime between September 5th and 10th the local Việt Cộng and NVA will *attack and take the National Police station at all costs.* It was an account to be taken seriously.

We captured this silver halide photo of "Uncle Hồ" on an operation just after his death.

In the wake of a now heightened alert condition, I scrounged two seventy-two-inch-long engineer stakes (sometimes called *U-shaped pickets*). I secured a defensive M18A1 claymore mine at the top of each stake, already hammered into in the moat mud east of our advisor's hooch. I was beginning to see how useful the Mines and Demolitions classes at Engineer OCS could be; they were paying off bigtime.

In this case, setting up the claymores meant driving the stakes down through three feet of mud slurry topping a thick, gooey sediment so that the Claymore mines peered just above the surface. This was exactly what I wanted. The mines would be much harder for attacking enemy sappers to see and avoid. I placed the blasting caps in the two mines electrically in series and ran the ignition wire with the M57 firing device back to our ammo bunker.

However, this was not a task of joy. The compound moat was much more than a simple moat. It was also the sewage repository for everyone who lived in the compound.

The claymore setup results satisfied me. But while the predicted enemy attacks did not materialize, the Claymore mines were not with us for long. A visiting MAT team NCO was in our ammo bunker scrutinizing our stockpile of weapons. While he swore he had nothing to do with it, the mines violently exploded at exactly that time. The back blast from the two Claymores blew in a part of our dining area wall. This unnamed man was thereafter affectionately referred to among team members as SFC Claymore.

The moat during the dry season. The grass has been burned to deny any approaching sappers cover.

Probably as a reaction to the death of Hồ Chí Minh, the Việt Cộng blew up this Bailey bridge a few klicks down Thunder Road from our compound on September 11, 1969.

Bailey Bridges are widely used truss bridges because they are portable, flexible, and easy to construct and deconstruct. The basic bridge component, the pane, is a six-man carry of 577 pounds that can be set up in many configurations, bridging spans from twenty to two hundred feet.

An engineer from the US 2/60 battalion advised us the Việt Cộng sappers most likely floated about 150 pounds of TNT on a raft under the bridge and command detonated it. Since TNT is a slower burning (heaving) charge as contrasted with a cutting charge like C4 plastic explosive, the force of the explosion lifted the bridge into the air, destroying it as it crashed back to the ground.

The roadside bunker by the bridge shown here was protected by barbed wire and punji stakes to discourage Việt Cộng sappers from approaching. It protected the men inside to some degree, but not the bridge they were guarding.

Chapter 12
In War, Shit Happens

Accidents occur with surprising frequency in war. Losses by either side inflicted upon themselves are known as friendly fire. A surprisingly large percentage of casualties is reported to result from such actions.

While out on Thunder Road in Tân Trụ, an artillery branch officer attached to the 2/60 was demonstrating to us his target registration points. These were pre-planned artillery strike coordinates that greatly eased quick and accurate artillery fire on a specific area once a *fire mission* was called for.

Unfortunately, in calling for the test fire mission, the officer transposed the coordinates telling us to *look over here.* We, having quickly realized his mistake, looked over *there* where the illumination marker round did explode. This ordinarily would be no more than a mild embarrassment to the captain. Major Gravett, the district senior advisor, had pointedly called down the mistake as one I, then a second lieutenant, had picked up on. But it turned out to be sadly predictive.

Months later, when calling in artillery against a nearby enemy, this same officer transposed coordinate digits with fatal results. The round accidentally impacted a Vietnamese peasant's thatched hut and killed him instantly. They took no action against the officer. Honest errors happen in war, and the incident was forgiven by the

Vietnamese district chief as part of the cost of the business of war. Thiếu tá (Major) Nguyệt was respected as a capable Vietnamese officer and leader who worked well with Americans.

Tân Trụ District Chief Nguyễn Nguyệt

While I was not a witness to the following tragedy, it occurred on September 17, 1969, in Tân Trụ district about eight klicks west of our compound. It did not take long for the word to get around that a Command and Control helicopter went down after a collision with another chopper. It was not due to hostile action.

This photo, while not of the accident being discussed, is in Tân Trụ district and serves to illustrate a troop extraction in progress with a Command and Control helicopter and a Cobra gunship like those in the accident. The crash occurred when the C&C chopper was climbing. It entered the orbit and collided with a Cobra gunship preparing to make a rocket run. All ten US personnel on both aircraft were killed.

Crew members were First Lieutenant Richard Snowdon, Warrant Officer Robert Mayer, SP5 William Fitch, and SP5 Gary Haught. The passengers were officers from the 9th Infantry Division's Third Brigade. Captain Donald Dietz, Major Dana Mitchell, 5/60 Battalion Commander Lieutenant Colonel Leo Sikorski, Major David Mackey, Major William McNair, and the brigade commander Colonel Dale Crittenberger.

The theme of this story is delayed intelligence delivery. The subsequent fixer is Captain "Buck" Manis from US Military Assistance Command, Việt Nam (MACV) Headquarters at Pentagon East near Sài Gòn. He was here visiting our district compound, hand-delivering intelligence reports on a near daily basis in late spring 1970. This is why:

It was toward the end of my tour. As the Phoenix advisor, I received intelligence from many sources. Much of it, frankly, was not actionable. About once a week, I would receive written intel reports in the mail distribution from MACV indicating a Who, What, When, Where scenario about the enemy. Seldom were these reports specific. Even more rarely were they accurate.

I received one report that was specific about the place and date the Việt Cộng were going to attack. It was a remote Vietnamese outpost in the village of An Nhựt Tân, a historical Việt Cộng stronghold that gave heavy casualties to Alpha Company of the US 2/60 in 1967.

It saddened me to read this detailed intelligence report. It was dated three weeks earlier, and the attack had occurred as predicted—just a week previously. The intelligence was spot-on. But the intelligence delivery system had failed.

It was particularly damaging because one of the most promising young Vietnamese officers in our district was killed in that attack.

Captain Buck Manis, MACV Headquarters, standing in front of our compound guard tower

Clearly, the attack could have been thwarted had the intelligence report arrived in a timely fashion.

So, being of brass balls, I wrote on the back of the report the date I received it, the date of the attack, and who was killed. I folded it into the shape of a paper airplane—all it was good for—popped it into a distribution envelope, and sent it back to MACV Headquarters.

I think they got the message. Within a few weeks, Captain Buck Manis was to the rescue, making regular trips by jeep, hand-delivering intel reports to us that were hot off the press.

Chapter 13

Good Intelligence:
Those Were the Days

The quality of intelligence was everything in war. Expending assets without making enemy contact as anticipated was wasteful and risky. Good intelligence was the difference between a directed fighting force and a pinball operation where the friendly troops simply caromed from place to place, blindly encountering whatever was there.

Critical to a successful targeting operation, such as with Phoenix ops in planning a raid or ambush, was the local tactical situation. Here, the Vietnamese held a deep understanding. They knew many villagers by name, who among them was sympathetic to the Việt Cộng, and their likely armament. This information was usually correct, but there were times, although infrequent when we were surprised by more enemy firepower and in greater numbers than expected. Sometimes we were surprised by less.

Another consideration was specific knowledge of the target environment: details on the terrain, any expected unusual weather, and both natural and man-made hazards such as red ant infestations and heavy agents' orange and white defoliated areas. The best defense against environmental hazards was to have local Vietnamese in on the planning and execution of the mission. American units employed *tiger scouts*. Some were former Việt Cộng who were quite willing to apply their expertise in action against their ex-brothers in arms. Vietnamese units, such as our Phoenix force, had homeboy Vietnamese who knew the locale well.

The Tân Trụ Phoenix men had insight into their home neighborhoods, of course, helping us avoid the biological plagues of the feared red ants and bees. Red ants, in my unfortunate experience, were the only natural phenomenon capable of inducing me to ignore enemy fire and, standing in place in whatever the tactical situation, put down my weapon to remove the ants as quickly as possible.

The *apis dorsata* or giant honeybee of Asia, producing nests several feet across, was feared for their ferocity and lethality. It was regarded as "the most ferocious and deadly stinging insect on Earth." The bees could stop a firefight, as both sides would withdraw from the immediate vicinity. Stings of this insect, focused on the head of the victim, left fist-sized welts, grossly distorting the appearance of the soldier, and interfering with his vision when close to the eyes.

An Apis Dorsata nest, common to Long An province in Việt Nam. Photo used with permission under CCAL, © 2017 Koeniger N, et al (2017). PLoS ONE 12(11).

On one occasion, we walked by a small tree with a nest of the bees, stinging two of our men who were walking ahead of me. The bees buzzed my head, and I quickly swiped them and sprinted away, knocking my glasses down into the surrounding mud. I felt helpless then because my vision was so poor; I could not see well enough to retrieve my glasses. One man of Intel grabbed them for me. There were smiles all around because Thiếu úy had lost his glasses.

Phoenix fighters in Tân Trụ were usually either conducting a raid or setting up an ambush. We mounted raids when we received information that a member of the Việt Cộng Infrastructure was operating in a rural hamlet. We would often be inserted by helicopter and quickly apprehend the civilian enemy. About half the time, the enemy would not resist, trying to talk their way out of it as if they were a citizen loyal to the government of South Việt Nam. Having local Vietnamese questioning the civilian paid a big dividend in these cases. They could tell when someone was falsely claiming to be merely a local rice farmer.

However, sometimes the target would run or immediately fire at us. This happened frequently when the VCI was a tax collector who carried the telltale payment records and occasionally was accompanied by one or two Việt Cộng soldiers.

In one case that comes to mind, early in my tour, we had targeted a VCI tax collector. She was going about her business, visiting each grass hut in the hamlet, collecting taxes on behalf of the Việt Cộng. We had American Recon members from the 2/60 with us, and as we walked into the hamlet, we saw movement and heard rustling in a nearby thicket. A Recon soldier fired a burst of M-16, 5.56 mm ammo into the brush. I heard an anguished "aaahhhhh" sound. He ordered her to put down any weapon she held and come out. There was no response, so another member of Recon, closer to the thicket, fired an M-79 HE round at the sound source. She was again ordered to come out. After a minute with no response, we moved up on the brush and found her body. Her skull had been cracked open with the appearance of a parted coconut shell. No weapon was recovered, but Vietnamese money, known as *đồng*, was confiscated.

Ambushes were a different story. Conducted at night almost exclusively, the Phoenix soldiers would quietly walk into an area offering troop cover such as nipa palm, set up a group of men in position for an expected appearance by a member of the VCI we had specifically targeted, and wait. When the enemy appeared, depending upon conditions, we would either open fire on them or attempt their capture.

The daylight raid pictured below involved more soldiers than usual because the target area required more coverage. The photos sequence the denouement—the extraction from the PZ after the raid had completed. Here, an unsuccessful one.

This uncommon sequence of photographs illustrates the troop pickup. Note the Command and Control helicopter and the Cobra gunship overhead. The gunship was cover for the troops and the extraction choppers and discouraged enemy action while the men were most vulnerable. The Command and Control chopper directed the activity to ensure coordination among aircraft and ground forces.

In the first photo's foreground: SP5 John Mullenax, our medic and particularly good tactical man. In the background of the second photo: Major Ray Gravett, district senior advisor for Tân Trụ. Insertion and extraction of friendly forces was choreographed carefully to minimize the period of vulnerability to the enemy and eliminate accidents. Despite the great care taken in establishing and executing protocols for these operations, helicopter accidents, as discussed earlier, occurred that resulted in a loss of life.

On another, more fruitful operation, we received intelligence indicating a lone VCI was operating in a remote place out of Tân Trụ's left testicle, the geographic oddity of a ball-shaped peninsula fashioned by the meandering Vàm Cỏ Tây river. The testicles were areas of marshy lowlands, made so by their proximity to the waterway. As the crow flies, they were but about five klicks distant from our Tân Trụ compound. They were sparsely populated with major strips of nipa palm as shown in this photo of the right testicle, just to the east of the left testicle.

To us and the rural riceroots people of Tân Trụ, including at least one 2/60 platoon leader, these were our *boonies*: relatively remote, sparsely populated, and at one time a haven for enemy forces. But now, toward the end of my tour, approaching mid-1970, large numbers of Việt Cộng forces were no longer in play here. However, VCI did still regard this as their home by trying to swim with the fish.

*The neck and most of the body of the Right Testicle of Tân
Trụ just below the Thumb in a neighboring district*

Air assaults or *insertions* were usually an effective method of
our attacks because we could put down in an area and place a
platoon-size element quickly on the ground. The downside was that
our transports, the ubiquitous and beloved UH-1H Hueys, could
be heard coming from many klicks away. The mitigation against
us heralding our approach was for the choppers to fly in a huge
circular pattern, making it difficult for the enemy to guess where
we would set down. The first photo shows the shadows of four of
the five Hueys in an insertion pattern before we approached the
left testicle. Rice paddies and thatched huts are evident along with
banana plants and nipa palm beside the riverbank.

The second photo is peering directly down on an irrigated
rice field with a raft of ducks near several thatched and tin-roofed
dwellings. After about twenty minutes circling in the air, the lead
chopper began the descent from several hundred feet flying altitude
into a rice paddy near the target hamlet. This was not considered a
"hot LZ." The door gunners raised their M-60s to meet any incoming
enemy fire, but as expected, we met no resistance going in.

As we quickly un-assed the choppers, we moved toward cover while the door gunners continued to hold their M-60s at the ready to discourage an enemy response. Our sudden appearance in the left nut surprised a local VCI who broke into a run, away from our LZ. The Phoenix men were right on him and he was quickly captured with minimal firing. Interestingly, a piece of metal fashioned as a

sign was visible directly inside a thicket of brush, nailed to a tree, warning of "DENGAR" (DANGER). It was red, capitalized letters on a sheet of metal the size of a loose-leaf piece of paper. Why the attempt at English? Possibly to lure souvenir-hunting Americans into the brush, which may have held booby traps. I did not intend to find out and gave the prospective souvenir a pass.

We interrogated the captured VCI. He finally agreed to take us to his cache. As the photo shows him emptying it, he built it from a large, buried coarse water jar.

Its intended use was to hold harvested rainwater since wells were uncommon in villages and those that did exist were often contaminated with arsenic, iron, manganese, or ammonium. The second photo shows two peasant children standing next to a line of water jars for comparison.

But this was more than a cache. It could hide an enemy in a pinch, even for extended periods of time, with support from his comrades or family. The Việt Cộng medals taken from the cache were, according to the inscription awarded to, among others, a Brave Killer of Americans. The belt buckle, which I had chrome plated, is believed to be NVA and it is unclear why it was held by a Việt Cộng guerrilla.

As my tour progressed, I naturally became more comfortable in my role as intelligence advisor. I understood I was not assigned to be a front-line troop, but as I have already discussed, I was part of the Intel team and I felt an obligation to them. One concern I had, though, in going to the field was my identity in this war: my Phoenix advisor job, my branch of service, and my rank. I had learned through reports that intelligence officers, particularly Phoenix types, were sought by the enemy. Further, one document we captured mentioned the resident Phoenix officer in the Tân Trụ compound and where he lived.

To give myself more protection in the highly unlikely event of capture, and to remain as tactically anonymous as possible, I only occasionally wore rank or branch insignia. When I did wear rank, I sometimes substituted the branch insignia of Infantry in place of that of Military Intelligence. It seemed a reasonable precaution to take, and no one expressed a concern about or objection to it.

Perhaps the greatest disappointment I have relating to intelligence was our inability to locate and capture Trần văn Thiệt, the Tân Trụ section chief. He was the big fish who got away. As is commonplace in Vietnamese culture, he was colloquially known by his birth position within his family. He was child number six, or *sáu*, so his familiar name was Sáu Thiệt. He was a powerful man in the district, but always seemed to be a step ahead of us in our planning.

In the earlier days of my tour, I tried test-carrying different weapons on operations, a not uncommon activity of soldiers in the field. The oddest I carried into the field was an M3A1 submachine gun, colloquially known as a *grease gun*. Introduced late in World War II, it replaced the Thompson submachine gun. It chambered a .45 Auto (11.43×23 mm) cartridge. I found it too heavy and with limited ammunition for my use. I took it into the field once, though I liked the short barrel, which made it easy to maneuver when I tried to interleave myself through a growth of nipa palm thicket.

The next weapon I carried was an M-79 grenade launcher often called a *bloop gun*. I had an affinity for this weapon; it felt naturally right for me. I carried primarily high-explosive (HE) rounds, although shotgun pellet rounds were also available. Unfortunately, my time with the M79 was short-lived. On the related operation, we encountered a Việt Cộng trying to escape us, requiring us to move as quickly as possible, almost at a run through a nipa palm and banana plant area. Looking ahead of me on the run, I saw the escaping enemy. I stopped, chambered a round in the M-79, and shot after him. But the round hit a low-hanging branch and exploded some twenty-five yards ahead of me, close to a member of our Intel force. Although he was not wounded, he was hit with shrapnel from my HE round. The men of Intel found this funny, but at the time, I did not. I decided I was not yet skilled enough to use this weapon safely and effectively.

After the M79 incident, I asked friends at the US 2/60 battalion if they could loan me what we knew as a CAR-15. It was an eleven-inch short-barreled (yes!) M-16 with an oversized flash suppressor. It used the same 5.56 mm ammunition and was highly sought after by troops who had to deal with thick brush or nipa palm. However, these specialized weapons were in short supply. I would have taken one away from a member of Recon, something I did not intend to do. After all, my charge was not as an assault or reconnaissance soldier. I was here to advise on intelligence matters, not engage the enemy as an infantryman. My standard issue M-16 would be my weapon. I fired it only when necessary, and it never failed me by jamming.

On another operation, we targeted a Việt Cộng who had guard responsibilities for local VCI. We were confident we could get this guy. The intel was good, and snatching him up, we thought, should be a rather quick operation. But when we arrived at the area he was expected to occupy, we could not find him. Conditions were poor. It was the rainy season and there was thick mud everywhere. After an hour of searching, we gave up on finding him and returned to our base camp.

A month later, there was a sweep operation in that area by a main force ARVN unit. By sheer luck, they encountered our guy, grabbed him, and brought him in for questioning. The captured Việt Cộng told the district chief during his interrogation that when Intel came through his area a month earlier, he hid in deep mud covered with dried nipa palm branches. One member of Intel stepped on his arm without realizing the Việt Cộng was hiding there. The district chief got a kick out of this. I liked his sense of humor.

As I had mentioned earlier, one of the Intel men was little more than a killer, a former Việt Cộng member who would wantonly shoot nearly anything—people, ducks, it did not seem to matter. We were moving into a hamlet where we had heard the enemy was operating. Two Việt Cộng were spotted, and we rushed after them. One of them was near me and ran through a thicket and out the other side. When he saw he could not outrun us, he stopped, dropped his weapon, and threw up his hands.

The killer Intel man brought his weapon to the ready, and pulled and released the charging handle, chambering a round. He intended to shoot the unarmed enemy. When the Việt Cộng saw this, he turned and bolted but immediately fell into a small pond. As he struggled to slosh through the chest-deep water, the killer fired a burst at him with his M-16 rifle from about ten feet away. At least some rounds impacted the man as he tried to climb the opposing bank of the pond, hitting him in the upper back, beneath his neck. He jerked suddenly and stiffly, sinking beneath the water. A few minutes later, when other members of Intel caught up to us, I explained where the enemy body was. One man entered the pond, reached down in five feet of water, and grabbed the dead man by his hair, pulling him up and out of the pond.

Some ops I went on were not productive in capturing or killing an enemy but had jocular aspects to them. A chopper inserted a squad of us into a lush area, the blades of grass being about two feet high, as I recall. The helicopters had no sooner lifted out when voices of excitement moved among the men. My first thought was that it was an unexpected enemy encounter. The Intel guys were unflappable, not easily disturbed, and something had seized their attention. Then, I saw them racing a few steps in different directions through the grass as if they were after an animal. There was no enemy in the immediate area, apparently, so the chase was on. It continued for a few minutes until the critter was cornered and taken prisoner. They had captured a Javan mongoose! Technically, it was most likely the subspecies more frequently seen in Việt Nam, a *herpestes javanicus exilis*. One man kept it while the operation continued and eventually finished. We walked back to our compound, and I did not hear about the mongoose again. I presume they ate it, although being opportunistic feeders, mongooses themselves are highly effective warriors when used in the fight against rats and snakes.

In looking back at my in-the-field participation, as I have shared mostly in this chapter, I occasionally put down my intelligence documents for a walk in the wild. On a few of these ops I took my PX-purchased Topcon Super RE 35 mm camera, the reason I have such vivid photographs of my time in Việt Nam.

Besides the primary Vietnamese reaction force of Intel, I sought to go into the field with other Phoenix-related units and commanders. My op time included: ops with the combined force of Intel and 2/60 Recon, variously commanded by First Lieutenant

Some men of Intel.

Ron Pieper ("*Saddle up!*"), First Lieutenant Jeff Riek (killed in action on February 25, 1970), and possibly more than one NCO including SGT Ken Chapple (seriously wounded and transferred stateside). With the Vietnamese alone, ops with an RF/PF unit commanded by Dai-'uy Hoàn (wounded and awarded an American Silver Star); and ops with the Vietnamese Phoenix Intel squad based out of Tân Trụ commanded by my two counterpart lieutenants (one seriously wounded and transferred to a non-combat job) and two NCOs.

Of the whole of operations in which I took part, fifty years later I recall scenes from eleven that resulted in contact with the enemy and two more that involved friendly fire incidents. Overall, less than one-third of my operations resulted in combat action. Except for teams of highly specialized units, our yield or percentage of ops where contact was made was probably on par with many line units, Vietnamese or American.

Chapter 14

PSYOP

Psychological Operations—PSYOP—was strongly supported and promoted in the Viêt Nam War. General William Westmoreland, in 1964, remarked:

> Psychological warfare and civic action are the very essence of the counterinsurgency campaign here in Vietnam...you cannot win this war by military means alone.

His successor, General Creighton Abrams, and higher commands, including the White House, placed continuing emphasis on gaining advantage through the employment of psychological operations. The government of South Viêt Nam established the Chiêu Hoi program, offering a path for those who wished to rally to the government side, or at least stop fighting for the Viêt Cộng. They adopted the *hearts and minds* strategy, intending to exert influence over the enemy and their sympathizers through aural and visual messaging known in PSYOP jargon as *product*.

At the tactical level, US forces had a PSYOP group at battalions known as *S-5*. The US 2/60 in 1969 was no exception. However, many PSYOP commands found themselves without sufficient resources to effectively fulfill their mission. Higher command sometimes considered them a sideshow of the main event—war fighting. As an intelligence officer, I had received some training in PSYOP and learned that the ingenuity of the organization employing PSYOP weaponry was key.

I had contacted an officer from the 2/60 Battalion S-5 to get the lay of the land from him: what resources he had, tactics used, and results. The 6th PSYOP battalion, 4th Psychological Operations Group, out of Bien Hoa, supported him. As part of his walk-through, he played for me an audio piece broadcast over loudspeakers under a Huey helicopter on nighttime operations. It was unusually scary to hear, and this was my perception knowing what I was listening to in daylight, sitting in his office. He remarked that when it was played at night over Việt Cộng territory, the audio never failed to draw ground gunfire.

I had read an article in *The MACV Observer*, the Army newspaper distributed to advisors in Việt Nam, about a soldier who left behind Ace of Spades playing cards as his unit's *calling cards* for whenever they encountered in combat, either Việt Cộng or North Vietnamese Army regulars.

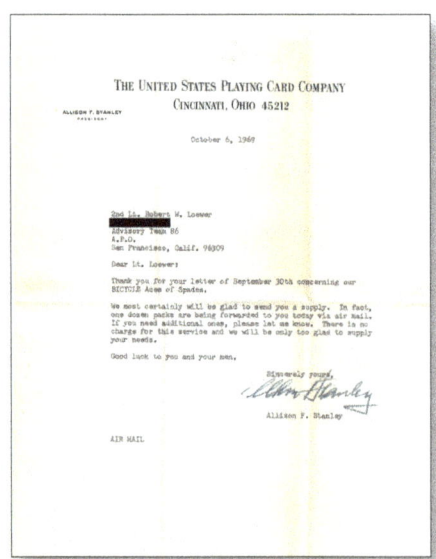

PSYOP

There was limited PSYOP practiced by the Vietnamese at our district. So, to leverage every tactical possibility to our advantage, I wrote a letter to the president of the United States Playing Card Company requesting a dozen decks of Ace of Spades playing cards for our use as calling cards. As the letter from Mr. Allison F. Stanley shows, he was pleased to honor the request for this product.

But not all tactics worked out. The effort was tried but judged by a Phoenix Intel squad sergeant and me to be callous in practice. It was a measure that would likely be interpreted as cruel and turn neutral nationalistic villagers against us. It could shape their interest to oppose offering information about local Việt Cộng activities. That would be too costly a trade-off. We dropped consideration of this idea. It was a worthwhile effort, but probably would not be productive for us.

The US and Vietnamese military had no corner on PSYOP activity. The Việt Cộng produced fliers and newspapers as well. Here is page one of the eight-page newspaper of issue #25, January 1, 1969, the *South Viet Nam In Struggle*, published in English by the "South Viet Nam National Front for Liberation Information Commission." It was probably produced west of III Corps in Ba Tu, Cambodia, also known as the Parrot's Beak. We captured this document in one of our raids targeting a member of the Việt Cộng Infrastructure.

It was fascinating to capture a document, in this case a newspaper, written in the English language. In my entire year in Tân Trụ, I faced only one enemy who spoke some English. A middle-aged man, a former teacher, took advantage of the Chiêu Hồi program and rallied to the side of the government of South Việt Nam. Encountering a language other than Vietnamese was a rarity. Many of the older Vietnamese, however, spoke some French as well as Vietnamese.

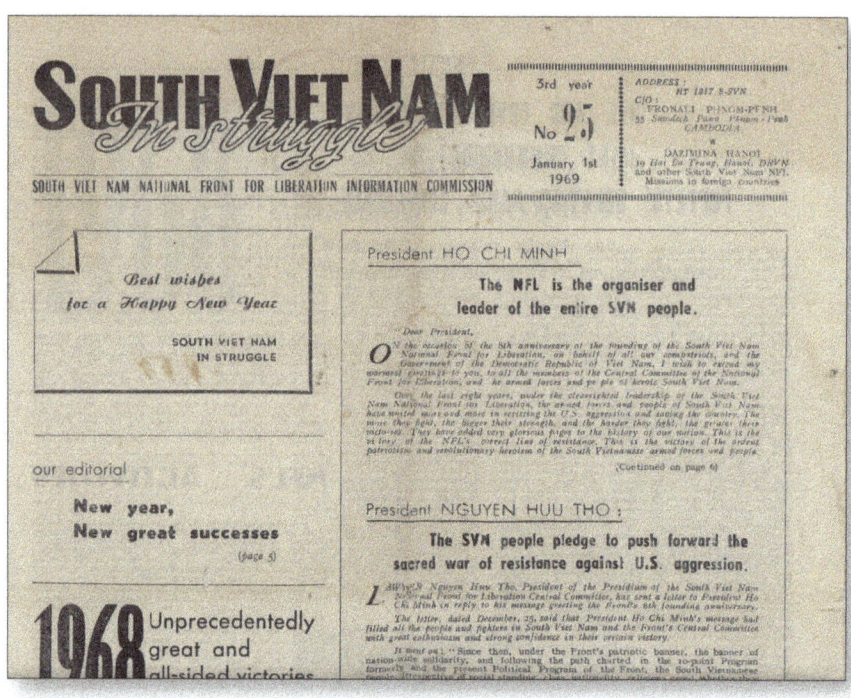

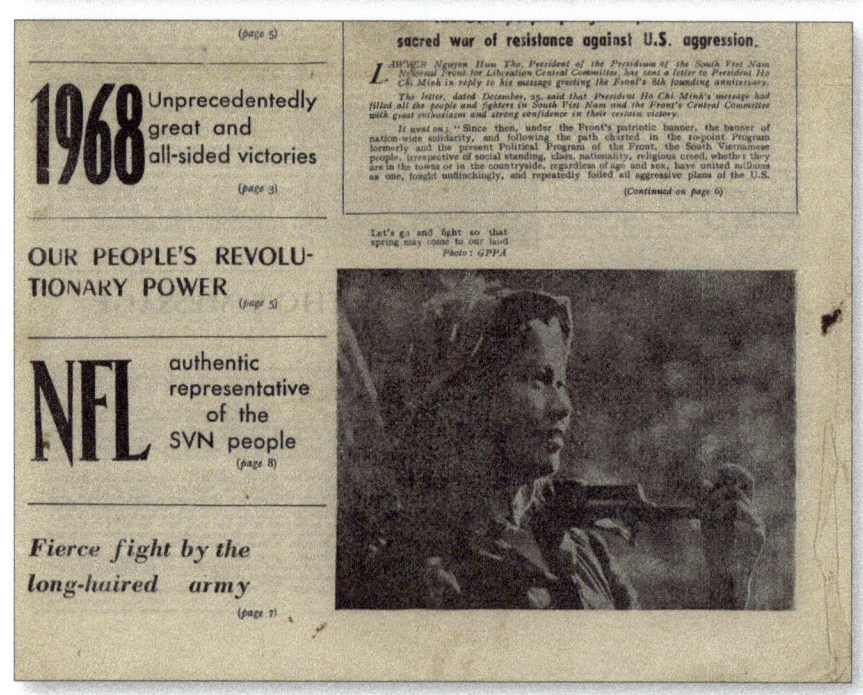

Chapter 15

He Said, She Said

Joseph Alsop, Sr.

In Joseph Alsop, Sr.'s nationally syndicated column, an article "Holes in the VC Apparatus" on the Việt Cộng in Tân Trụ, appeared in the April 3, 1970 issue of *Stars and Stripes*, a US-published newspaper in Việt Nam for GIs. Alsop appeared a slow-moving crusty sort as the district senior advisor and I sat down with him.

It was an informal briefing, more of a serious chat than anything else. Alsop struck me as having a preconceived idea of the Việt Cộng in Tân Trụ. At first, he seemed more interested in having his view confirmed by us than learning what we knew. However, his opinion of the activities of the Việt Cộng Infrastructure (VCI)—the Việt Cộng government—in Tân Trụ district, Long An province, and more widely in Sub Region 3 were not inconsistent with our intelligence. The NVA were indeed filling some positions in the Việt Cộng units. He was correct on that point. But I did not believe the NVA, who in some key ways were not appreciated by the Việt Cộng, would take positions in the shadow government of the Việt Cộng Infrastructure. Alsop's speculation was not borne out by our observations. That included us noticing the local peasantry, who while sympathetic to the Việt Cộng, often would not bury NVA who were killed in action even when they were fighting in the same unit alongside their relatives.

Lieutenant General Michael Davison

During the second quarter of 1970, Lieutenant General Michael Davison had been assigned command of the II Field Force in Viêt Nam. Concurrently, the general also became responsible for conducting Nixon's Cambodian Campaign, an incursion intended to capture the communist troop's headquarters, the Central Office for South Viêt Nam (COSVN). The campaign was a military move that was subsequently met with considerable public attention in the United States.

The commanding general's presence at some Phoenix Program offices in Long An province, southern III Corps, was to engage district Phoenix advisors and get their thinking on a couple of themes. The topics were enemy supply lines feeding from the neighboring Cambodia's Parrot's Beak peninsula border area into South Viêt Nam, and their impact on the Viêt Cộng Infrastructure neutralization effort that was Phoenix.

By Memorial Day, with less than two months before the completion of my tour, I had become familiar with that enemy corridor through both human intelligence and electronic sensor reports. They showed occasional troop and supply movement and some of the US interdiction efforts. As the Phoenix advisor, it fell to me to give a briefing at the Tân Trụ district compound to the CG and his staff.

At mid-morning, the briefing, held in our DIOCC office, was wrapping up. I judged that it had gone well. But I was never more surprised than a week later when I received the original note imaged here. The III Corps Phoenix staff had written up the general's laudatory comments about my presentation and the Q & A that followed. Further, the III Corps officer-in-charge, Colonel Krause, had asked for a brief follow-on study to provide more detail on Viêt Cộng resupply discussed in the briefing.

1.　　　LTC Knittle – info 29-5-70

TO: 2.　　　Major Pollard – Action　　　　　　Date: 28 May

Yesterday while Gen Davison was in Long An (P), Cần Giuộc (D) it was mentioned that an alleged District Section Chief had rallied but they knew little about him, nor had much info been obtained on him. He has been sent to Province. Col Krause wants them to forward ASAP a report of what they were able to get out of this guy to the CG that they aren't all stupid down there. Therefore, get hold of Hemovich and tell him to send us a good debrief on this guy so that we can forward it to CG II FF. I'd say we ought to have it by COB Sun.

A related action came up on the trip as well. In Tân Trụ Lt Loewer did a great job and the CG was impressed very much (the most impressive thing in the trip). Loewer said the local VC resupplied about every 10 days. He was asked by Krause to prepare a short study on effects of Cambodia operation on the resupply of the local

VC. No time was ever given but we should remind them if we don't hear by about the 6th of June.

COL William L. Knapp
Tel: 4496

LT Col Thomas. I think this is completely out of line for a higher staff agency to coordinate and place requirements on a subordinate without using the CHAIN OF COMMAND.

Maj Barnett

My Advisory Team 86 supervisor, Major James Barnett, had a problem with the general's request. Barnett was a Special Forces guy who tended to be overly forceful. He did not appreciate the tasking order that he regarded as a clear chain of command violation. The Team 86 commander agreed with Barnett. Consequently, the opportunity for me to do work that Davison would see quickly melted away. But I could not be too upset with Barnett; I was getting short—less than sixty days left in country and, God willing, would be home soon. Although I did not know it

Major James Barnett, Tân Trụ district senior advisor during the second half of my tour

at the time, Davison apparently needed analysis help on Việt Cộng resupply from Cambodia and, depending on how my report was received, I might have become a "volunteer" for a tour extension. Thank you, Major Barnett!

The Texas major had a light-hearted side, though. I recall once in idle conversation when he was referring to a singer and used only the first name Buck. I am not a big country music fan, but everyone has heard of Buck Owens. I saw an opportunity to tease so I grabbed it. "Buck who?," I inquired. His response? "Thiếu úy, that will reflect," he joked in retaliation, referring to my Officer Evaluation Report (OER).

The originator of the abovementioned memo was Colonel William Knapp, later to be the author of *Phoenix/Phung Hoang and the Future: A Critical Analysis of the US/GVN Program to Neutralize the Việt Cộng Infrastructure*, available on Amazon.

Pictured below are two Long An province Phoenix officers I knew. To my knowledge they did not get into the field often, illustrating the point that even Phoenix advisors' duties and risks varied widely. On the left is CPT Mike Hemovich, mentioned in COL Knapp's note.

Ambassador Robert Komer

Bob Komer began in 1967 to build the huge civilian pacification organization of CORDS (Civil Operations and Revolutionary Development Support) in Việt Nam. Komer was credited with the brilliant move of placing CORDS under the military to satisfy their view of a unified command but controlled by civilians.

Komer was making the rounds through the seven Phoenix Program district offices (DIOCCs) in Long An province to judge their effectiveness. His tour with each was in concert with Lieutenant General Davison's investigative charge from Richard Nixon. The president wanted Davison to determine the extent of Cambodian supply lines—in particular, the Hồ Chí Minh Trail egress into Việt Nam at the peninsula west of Sài Gòn known as Parrot's Beak.

He appeared at the Tân Trụ DIOCC one afternoon and received a thorough briefing from the Vietnamese Phoenix team. Komer had visited five or six DIOCCs before coming to Tân Trụ. He appeared satisfied as he walked out of the facility toward me at the advisor end of the compound. Not knowing his reputation, his brevity and directness surprised me.

His remarks lasted only a few minutes, but he pointedly gave our Phoenix office the highest marks, indicating that most DIOCCs "… did not work well…" while the Tân Trụ DIOCC did. He finished by crediting us with the "…best in the province" operation. No small amount of praise from the ambassador and well deserved by the Vietnamese Phoenix staff in Tân Trụ.

Vice President Nguyễn Cao Kỳ

Our district compound was being inspected by none other than the flamboyant and reputedly corrupt Nguyễn Cao Kỳ, vice president and former Air Force general of South Việt Nam. It is believed Kỳ was instrumental in arranging the bogus Việt Nam elections of 1965 and was quoted as saying he favored "the way Hitler had ruled Germany."

When Kỳ's chopper landed, and the group disembarked, his aide remarked that they would return to the helicopter in fifteen minutes. His aircraft was sitting on our pad, rotor idling, when a Vietnamese child who had stepped on a live M-79 grenade launcher round was brought into our advisor hooch in the compound. Answering their request for help, we called for a dustoff medical evacuation helicopter, which was a common response for a seriously wounded person, military or not. Having the lowest priority for a medical evacuation, though, there were no choppers available to take the child to a hospital in Tân An City, about ten minutes flying time from us.

> M-79 weapons, commonly called *bloop guns* because of the sound they made when fired, shot "grenades" of different types distances of up to about four hundred yards. High-explosive, shotgun (pellet), CS (tear) gas, and illumination were some types of rounds available. Occasionally, the HE rounds would not explode when they impacted but would detonate later when someone—often playing children—stepped on or picked them up.

Unknown to Kỳ or his entourage, Kỳ's helicopter pilot, an American, had overheard us on the radio receiving the bad news of helicopter unavailability. He keyed his mic and spoke up, volunteering to take the child to Tân An. I quickly okayed it. The child was put on the chopper and was on its way. About five minutes later, Kỳ emerged from our hooch, ready to leave the area. He discovered his chopper was gone and could not be back for another fifteen minutes. Let us say he was somewhat upset. The Vietnamese vice president was not used to being kept waiting.

After his helicopter returned to the compound from its mercy mission and Kỳ finally departed, Colonel Sanderson, senior-most advisor in Long An province, leaned over to me. Sanderson questioned, "I guess you could not hear the aide saying they would return in fifteen minutes due to Kỳ's helicopter rotor noise, Lieutenant Loewer?" I smiled and nodded. I was off the hook. Sanderson was the best.

One of the finest officers and true gentlemen I have known, not at all rank-conscious, Brigadier General Alfred Sanderson died in the spring of 2017. He was considered to be a warm-hearted officer with an engaging smile. In Viêt Nam, he took an interest in this young officer and suggested to my district senior advisor, after an action in May 1970, that I be considered for the third highest armed forces decoration. In no way did I merit this award. It may have been suggested to him by an excited subordinate who accompanied me on the operation, but I appreciated the sentiment and personal recognition from a man like Sanderson. A brief bio on the general:

May 15, 1928 - Mar. 27, 2017

Brigadier General Alfred Sanderson, age eighty-eight, made his hometown in Stockton, California. General Sanderson attended the United States Military Academy at West Point. His military career of thirty years in the US Army ran from 1950 through 1980. "Sandy" retired in 1980 as a brigadier general. He was an infantry combatant in both Korea and Viêt Nam. His decorations included

Silver Star
Bronze Star
Distinguished Flying Cross
Eleven Air Medals
Purple Heart
Combat Infantryman's Badge
Master Parachutist Badge

George D. Jacobson

During the week of April 6, I had yet another briefing. The assistant chief of staff for CORDS, (Colonel) George D. Jacobson attended with the foreign bureau editor for *The New York Times*, whom at this writing I believe to have been Robert B. Semple, Jr. They came to Tân Trụ to get the latest on the tactical situation.

As with other visiting dignitaries, they were particularly interested in enemy supply lines coming from sanctuaries in Cambodia. Both the Parrot's Beak and Fishhook areas supported major enemy supply depots. Semple's lengthy front-page headline article in *The New York Times*, "Nixon Sends Combat Forces to Cambodia to Drive Communists from Staging Zone," published nearly four weeks later discusses the Nixon decision to interdict protected resupply lines through a Cambodian incursion.

https://www.nytimes.com/1970/05/01/archives/nixon-sends-combat-forces-to-cambodia-not-an-invasion-president.html

Brigadier General Camp

We were holding a rare award ceremony in our district compound, principally for the benefit of our Vietnamese counterparts, to give them American medals for bravery. They were referred to then as *impact awards*. These were regular issue US Army valor medals, but in this scenario suggested by higher command, they awarded the medals immediately following the action. This was intended to quickly recognize the Vietnamese contribution and encourage further independent action on their part. The justifying paperwork for the awards would come later. On this day, a few Americans, myself included were receiving awards.

We asked for a general to do the honors to reinforce our view that recognizing Vietnamese bravery was especially important to Americans. Brigadier General Camp was at the top of the duty roster (generals did not like to come to Tân Trụ, I was told) so his UH-1H

BG Camp at a US 2/60 award ceremony

Huey helicopter came in with four rifle-bearing, spit-shined soldiers in accompaniment. So far, so good. When he got to me, he leaned in and said, "Loewer, a lot of people do not understand the Phoenix Program," expressing support for the work done. But as the general walked further down the line pinning on the medals, 50-caliber machine gun fire in short bursts whizzed just over our heads.

In a hilarious sequence, the general's four starched fatigue guards, acting surprised and unsure of what to do, ran from the compound to his chopper and laid down alongside it with rifles pointed in different directions. Perhaps to ensure the general's route of escape remained available? I am not certain.

Anyway, we soon learned the shots interrupting the award ceremony came from an Air Cushioned Vehicle of the US 2/60 Battalion. They occasionally employed these hovercraft for easier traversing of the Delta rice paddies. This time, they were apparently reconning by fire on the opposite side of a small, nipa palm-lined river two klicks away. The 2/60 men were careless, the general's staff was aghast, and we were quietly laughing our butts off.

Chapter 16
Our Neighbor Is Overrun

B elow is a photo taken from our (Vietnamese) compound tower, whose defensive equipment included an M60 machine gun, a searchlight, and a hand cranked siren. When the siren wailed, the guards believed we were under attack. That sound of imminent danger I, unfortunately, still remember well today.

The Tân Trụ district compound tower was sometimes also manned by US snipers seeking the Việt Cộng, who were always more active at night. The snipers were highly qualified and would hit targets more than a klick away with their scoped and specially precisioned M-14 rifles.

The Vietnamese artillery base beyond the unpaved
Thunder Road and pond

Our contact with enemy sappers was once a rather close call, beyond the occasional probes we had to our compound. As the photo shows, out the front gate and a stone's throw across the dirt road and pond was a small Vietnamese two-tube artillery base. Sappers briefly overran it in a pre-dawn attack. In this photo I took from the district compound tower, it is visible above the Tổ Quốc Trên Hết (Homeland Above All) banner.

To say the aftermath was a grisly scene is to understate it. When I entered the artillery compound after daybreak, it was clear they had overrun it, however briefly. The survivors had completed the medical evacuation of the wounded, clearing of unexploded ordnance, and their assessment of the extent of the damage. A few dead enemy and friendly forces were lying about mostly as crumpled figures on the ground or wire, whatever their bodies encountered as they fell. The telltale marks of detonated explosives including enemy sapper satchel charges were evident.

As I walked through the compound, my eyes were pulled to something hanging from the Concertina—a razor wire used to establish military obstacles and highly effective in slowing down or stopping intruders. It was the body of a sapper who had run through the compound throwing his satchel charge at the Command and Control bunker. He had missed his target. But he made it to the opposite side of the perimeter wire on his way out when a burst of M-60 machine gun fire caught up with him. His body at the waist had been cut in half as his innards were splayed out into the air. The two halves of his body, each hanging almost vertically on different sides of the Concertina wire, were barely held together by his sinewy tendinous tissues and spine.

The attack had come just before dawn, when most everyone would still be asleep and slow to respond. It appeared to have been well-planned: they made entry on the north and east sides of the perimeter by slowly crawling through the mud and under the wire. When the sappers were past the wire and in close enough, they jumped up and ran for the command-and-control bunker, tossing one or more satchel charges at its entryway. As luck for friendly forces would have it, the enemy missed its target, leaving the command structure intact and giving the artillery base officers time to order a response, and to radio for additional support.

The dozen soldiers staying in our district compound responded by approaching from the south and ending the attack at that point. It is not known if there were other enemy forces hidden further north that may have been brought into play had the Command and Control bunker been destroyed. It is speculative to consider that a fully successful enemy attack on the Vietnamese artillery base would have been followed by continuing the ground attack to our district compound about a hundred yards away. But I was not the only one to whom this stray thought occurred.

Chapter 17

There Was Celebration
and Laughter

While Viêt Nam national holidays are often associated with attacks by the NVA and Viêt Cộng, Tet of 1968 being a widely publicized one, there was time taken by the South Vietnamese to celebrate these occasions when the tactical situation allowed.

As advisors to the Vietnamese, we would adapt some of our holiday celebrating to their holidays, and they would sometimes adapt their festivity to our holidays. After all, we lived together in the same compound, and it was a way to foster closer relationships, something we were always working to accomplish.

The cuisine was typically Vietnamese, the food of the host country. I had adjusted to some of the more unusual offerings to Americans such as duck heart, aorta and all. But I could not warm up to the tiết canh, or blood pudding. This tasty dish is prepared somewhat differently depending upon the locale in Viêt Nam. In Tân Trụ, the soldiers heated the freshly drawn duck blood, allowing it to coagulate into a pancake shape. They sliced it into half-inch strips and served it as a finger food.

The two most memorable holidays were Thanksgiving and Christmas. Christmas was a surprise to me because I did not realize the relatively large number of Christians within the South Vietnamese armed forces. Pictured on the previous page is a quiet ceremony held inside our district compound; it was more of a segregated holiday observance. The Vietnamese enjoyed their rather solemn activity, and we Americans got out our ritual Santa suits and asked the children what they wanted for Christmas. It was a perfect metaphor for the demeanor of the Vietnamese and Americans.

Well, mostly the children. Ah...the responsibilities of the lowest ranking officer. No, SFC Mosley did not get what he wanted for Christmas.

The revelry of Thanksgiving was another matter entirely. Some of us were still wondering what happened. It all started this way....

After enjoying a traditional Vietnamese Thanksgiving dinner, two American NCOs decided it would be entertaining to throw one another into a small moat. The body of water was located between our compound and the Vietnamese artillery compound, across the Tân Trụ primary but unimproved dirt road leading to Highway 4. Since we worked and lived closely with the Vietnamese, they were not unfamiliar with sporadic American pranks and humor. So, when a few advisors tossed each other in the water, looks of *those crazy Americans are at it again* surprised no one. They watched with mild amusement as the guys let it all hang out, or so they thought. But when the last lower-ranking American NCO had been thrown in, they did not realize the advisor's sense of humor monster had not yet been fully fed.

The junior NCOs set their sights on senior NCOs, grabbing and carrying the reluctant dunkees to the moat, and dropping them in the paddy water. Next came a few Vietnamese who were standing close by and starting to appreciate the humor of each successive senior NCO being pulled against his will to the moat. Followed by the junior officers, including me. Now, everyone could see the intended endpoints—the American major and the Vietnamese district chief.

While Major Gravett had a refined sense of humor, it did not always percolate to the surface. The district chief, Thiếu tá (Major) Nguyệt, was a local god to his men, and this sort of thing was not done. But the moment was seized, and the Vietnamese and Americans let their hair down in front of the compound officers and men.

It reminded us all of the value of team building, and we willingly posed for a photo of what could have been an embarrassing moment.

As I have discussed, the Vietnamese district compound where I lived was in the countryside, and the US 2/60 Battalion was located a couple of klicks away. Although rare, there were opportunities at the 2/60 compound for visiting entertainers to distract the troops from the war for a few hours. It depended on the tactical situation. Most

2/60 soldiers enjoying local entertainment on their bandstand.

of the time, however, it was too risky for performers to come to our area. Indeed, as mentioned earlier, a Vietnamese two-tube artillery site across the dirt road in front of our compound was overrun by sappers in early 1970. And in 1969 and 1970, our Vietnamese compound took mortars, rocket fire, and sapper probes in the wire from time to time.

So, while we advisors in relatively remote and unsecured locations did not qualify for visiting entertainment groups such as musicians, the US 2/60 occasionally did. Here is one such band visit I noticed as I was driving by the US unit at Camp Scott toward Tân An city about ten klicks away to get our mail.

Bob Hope did visit III Corps during my tour with his show at the Tân Sơn Nhứt air base a couple of hours' drive away. But the powers-that-were made it a requirement to wear a steel pot helmet to qualify being there. My guess is they wanted to reduce the massive interest in attending. Well, it worked. I wore a camouflage beret in the field and had no intention of changing my combat appearance, including requisitioning a helmet, even for Bob Hope.

Chapter 18
Dai-'uy (Captain) Greg Barker

As the Tân Trụ district Phoenix advisor and Intelligence officer, I enjoyed having assets and matériel available to me from the 2/60 Battalion commander in exchange for intelligence and tactical cooperation. Lieutenant Colonel William N. Ciccolo seemed uncomfortable settling into his new command, having recently replaced Lieutenant Colonel Gregory P. "Matt" Dillion, a well-respected officer whose visage could have been a poster boy for hard-driving army authority. Dillon liked to put himself out there, at risk with his troops, readily earning their admiration. It was a hard act to follow.

Ciccolo's leadership appeal was less obvious, his approach governed by a critical and more formal view in the management of the battalion. Despite his almost take-no-prisoners approach to command, Ciccolo and I had a favorable professional connection, probably due to the quality of intelligence I shared with their unit.

However, the lieutenant colonel's relationship with his S-2, Captain Greg Barker, was not yet one of mutual respect. Ciccolo, at an informal staff meeting held around a large circular table in the officer's club at the 2/60 base camp, mentioned something was amiss with Barker's reporting as I was walking in. My visit was fortuitous for Barker since I rarely went to the O Club. I took the opportunity to soften the blow for Barker since Ciccolo would not jump on me nearly as hard—I was not in his command. I offered, "You can blame me for that, sir." Ciccolo quickly smiled and responded with, "Okay, Lieutenant Loewer. I will!" to a chorus of laughter from the somewhat nervous officers. The tension of Barker's public smacking-in was bled off, lightening the moment, and his apparent faux pas was explained away. Mission accomplished.

Captain Barker and I got along well, although he was formal in our get-acquainted meetings. He came into Tân Trụ having recovered from serious wounds while in a command position with the Big Red One. I may have encountered him before. He apparently taught classes at the Fort Belvoir, Virginia OCS during the period I attended. Barker did two tours in Việt Nam.

Over time, Captain Barker relaxed when talking with me and proved to be amiable enough. It may have had something to do with the actionable intelligence I gave him. On one occasion, he used it to send helicopter gunships into an area of nipa palm. While no Việt Cộng were captured or killed, they observed multiple secondary explosions when the choppers rocketed the enemy bunkers, a strong indication enemy munitions were present.

Captain Greg Barker at his S-2 (Intelligence) desk at Camp Scott
(photographer unknown)

Barker liked to avoid personal conflict and, as we became better acquainted, was not hung up on rank in the opinion of this (then) first lieutenant. He had that compelling need for friendliness but strongly juxtaposed with friend-or-foe uncertainty and aloofness not uncommon among men shocked by combat. Judging by the degree of sandbagging in his jeep, though, it seemed overprotective. However, had I received his wounds, I may well have taken the same view.

Let me add a confession: I stole Greg Barker's idea of grease-penciling a weekly intelligence message for my team and called it, as he did, the *Crystal Ball*. The difference was he put his on the wall of the 2/60 TOC, hoping for interest. I put mine on the back of the advisor hooch's latrine door, where men who sat down would have no choice but to read it.

First Lieutenant Loewer meeting with Captain Barker

Sadly, though, Greg Barker was destined for misfortune and notoriety: after his Việt Nam tour, back in the World he was convicted of killing a woman in 1982 with a military .45 pistol. They met at the popular Rafters bar in Alexandria, Virginia. She subsequently rebuffed his amorous advances, leading, it is alleged, to his violence.

He escaped from Virginia authorities and began an eight-year run from the law, ending up in Las Vegas, involved in at least three bank robberies. Barker was finally caught in Nevada. That apprehension appeared on the April 24, 1991 episode of TV's *Unsolved Mysteries*. Barker's case was also profiled on *Most Wanted* with John Walsh. He was suspected of another murder in Fort Huachuca, Arizona in 1973. Apparently, law enforcement officials strongly believed he was a serial killer.

Barker was convicted of first-degree murder and bank robbery in 1992. He was sentenced to sixty years in prison—110 years with fifty years suspended. He accepted this plea deal to avoid the remote possibility of a death sentence. Barker subsequently appealed in 1993 but was not successful.

Barker spent time for the bank robberies at the supermax prison in Florence, Colorado along with exceptionally high-profile inmates including Zacarias Moussaoui (9/11 planner), Richard Reid (underwear bomber), Theodore Kaczynski (Unabomber), Terry Nichols (Oklahoma City bomber), Robert Hanssen (FBI agent guilty of espionage), and Joaquín Guzmán (El Chapo). In 2003, Barker was transferred to Virginia as inmate number 199179 to be incarcerated for the 1982 murder. Barker would have been eligible for parole in 2024 but he died a few years ago.

As a combat PTSD veteran, I occasionally consider how much Greg Barker's apparent illness contributed to his criminal behavior that was very much out of character with his Việt Nam professional persona. With due respect and sympathy to those whose lives he took and hurt, Captain Greg Barker was perhaps a combat casualty of a different kind.

Chapter 19
Reflecting, then Home

Less than a month now. I am so short I can hardly look over the tops of my boots. Pushing back from pizza bones, feeling satiated, will soon be part of my life again. My NCO counterpart told me *no more missions for you*. Well, Okay. I will live with that. And in truth, perhaps I will live because of that. SGT "P" is the man I thank.

The *Súng ngắn K-54* (type 54 handgun) is known colloquially as a *Black Star* pistol. It was a true trophy find during the Việt Nam War since it was worn only by high-ranking NVA officers and important Việt Cộng, usually key members of the Việt Cộng Infrastructure. While we encountered NVA in the Delta, our target was the VCI, and often the tax collectors among them carried K-54s.

Sergeant "P"

Late in my tour, my adopted counterpart SGT "P" and the boys gave this pistol to me as a *secret* for their advisor. The photo shows them returning from the op in which they got the K54. I would take back to my home in the States a lanyard (not shown), a leather holster, two magazines, and the K-54. Although the gift I received was authentic, I

The Intel squad getting a partial lift back from a productive operation in capturing a 7.62 x 25 mm caliber K-54

removed both sides of the black star hand grip before having it chrome-plated in Viêt Nam. Both plastic grips readily broke when removing them and have since been replaced with facsimiles. About eight years after I returned, I had married and was enjoying the company of my first child. I removed the handgun from my home and gave the K54 to my friend and business partner, Craig Denbrook. Craig has recently returned it and reports it still shoots!

SGT "P" and I meshed well. We had shared interests, of course, but beyond that we seemed to like one another. The differences of nationality and military rank did not impede mutual respect and

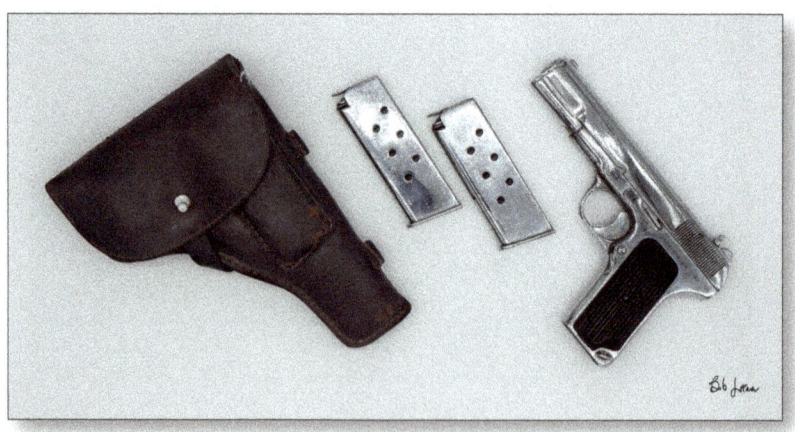

appreciation for one another's competence as warriors. "P" looked out for me, particularly in the early days of my tour when I was still wet behind the ears. He seemed to enjoy the differences between us, a maturity rarely seen in men our age.

We were both needed in the Tân Trụ TOC one afternoon to coordinate helicopter gunship attack runs on suspected Việt Cộng positions. We were sitting in chairs, relaying the radio calls in Vietnamese and English between the Vietnamese soldiers on the operation and the American Cobra gunship pilot. In a lull in the conversation, "P" leaned over and pulled the hair on my calf, watching it closely as he tested tugging on it. He was curious because Vietnamese men did not have much hair on their legs. It was commonplace among Americans, of course. And "P"'s action was another demonstration of our mutual comfort, informality, and friendship.

The replacement officers were coming into Tân Trụ with some regularity now. More intelligence branch types like me, but better trained. More Phoenix study and, importantly, with Vietnamese

Unidentified MAT member (L) and my Phoenix replacement,
First Lieutenant O'Brien

language school under their belts. They were better educated in Vietnamese customs and the need, as Americans, to stay in the background. The Việt Cộng propaganda of Americans lording their power over the Vietnamese "puppet" authorities was finally being spoken to more effectively with added cultural and language education. A pity it had not begun years earlier.

One of these replacements was First Lieutenant Rich Flanagan. There was no time, really, to get to know him, but I would have liked to do exactly that. He mentioned to more than a few people how much he loved Simon and Garfunkel's "Bridge Over Troubled Water."

First Lieutenant
Rich Flanagan

Looking back on my year of service of living among the Vietnamese in their district compound, I considered how effective the work we were doing was. On one hand, we had the US military might, extraordinarily effective in large-scale operations and targeted actions. The concept of CRIP, American Recon men teamed with Vietnamese Intel soldiers worked well in terms of body count and eliminating targeted enemy.

But the other war, the pacification effort, seemed to fall short. In the words of Bob Komer, head of CORDS, the major unified American and Vietnamese pacification effort, it was too little, too late. Perhaps, as Lieutenant Colonel Trần Ngọc Châu himself had suggested, indeed he initially misinterpreted, the enemy was the manifestation of underappreciated cultural divisions within Vietnamese society itself, which were permitted to fester and grow.

Eventually becoming malignant and spawning a riceroots revolutionary effort as far back as the French attempt at colonialism, it was there for all to see but unobserved by those in power.

As class differences heightened, rural unrest increased with anger directed at the central government. Opposition took to armed conflict, then guerrilla tactics trying to gain influence over the peasantry. The Communist North, seeing the opportunity, subverted the Southerners, many of whom simply wanted to maintain the traditional Vietnamese culture and whose political attitudes were no more than nationalistic.

In the opinion of this advisor, Châu was correct. The *other war* should have been addressed from the outset of American intervention and should have been a full-throated hearts-and-minds effort to solve the problems ensuing from the French colonialists' adventures. Accomplishing this mission would have taken from the Việt Cộng their ability to gain traction among the rural Vietnamese, driving them from swimming with the fish into the open and making for easier fodder for American military might.

Advisors could have been better trained in language and culture of the Vietnamese. Consideration could have been given to the personality of those selected for advisor positions to avoid assigning those who were naturally overbearing or who must always be *in charge*. Advisors could have been taught to work behind the scenes and to allow Vietnamese to take a more direct role.

It is a sad postscript that the US, having gone through the divisiveness of Việt Nam, Afghanistan, and other countries, does not support a genuine and full hearts-and-minds approach to meet its own interests by offering a helping hand to nations in need.

When there was time to reflect on it, the Việt Nam countryside could appear quite peaceful, contradicting its true nature, especially when viewing it from the air. Escaping the din of wartime ambiance even briefly was best accomplished by going on a visual reconnaissance (VR) by helicopter. And for this twenty-two-year-old, VRs were completely exhilarating. I requested the air assets when needed for reconnaissance and, while it was still part of the job observing an important land area for enemy activity, the sensation of pushing through the air at 150 mph at treetop level in a Loach helicopter was unmatched.

You will notice the vegetation in the background. This is the much talked about *nipa palm,* an extremely dense low-growing palm that allowed the enemy to hide great numbers of soldiers in a relatively small area. It was particularly dangerous because friendly troops could walk right up on the nipa without seeing potentially large numbers of enemy. It was one reason the US employed organophosphate defoliants such as agent orange, apparently without giving much thought to the consequences that would ensue decades later.

June 22 was a day of celebration. It was Vietnamese National Assistance Day where the Vietnamese thanked all foreign forces in Việt Nam for their backing by throwing a party. We called it *be kind to an advisor* day. I was one month from heading back across the pond to my home. The luncheon on this occasion was in my honor and although I eschewed formalities, I appreciated these men of the Intel squad whom I had come to know and respect as true brothers.

One man whom I saw occasionally in the compound (photo), but not a member of Intel, attended the going-away party. Sitting across the table from me, he noticed the ice in my drink had melted and grabbed a chunk of ice, putting it in my glass. "Dụ má," I responded, jokingly chiding him for refilling my glass with ice putatively against my wishes. My friend SGT "P" laughed loudly and holding an index finger in the air to emphasize  his point exclaimed "Perfix!," meaning my pronunciation of that common profane epithet among Vietnamese soldiers was dead on.

Toward the conclusion of the festivities, I judged there was an expectation I would speak to those who attended, so I responded to the interest with the appreciation in my heart. "I am only twenty-two and have much to learn, but the people of Việt Nam have taught me a great deal." I saw pondering faces around the table, and that concerned me. Later in the evening, after the get-together had broken up, I approached my interpreter, SGT "L". I shared my remarks and told him I thought I had fucked up. "No," he assured, with an appreciative smile. "You did okay."

As a point of interest, in the photograph's background is a red rotatable *fire arrow*, a crude but effective tool to aid in the defense against an enemy attack. Kerosene placed in the small tin cans is ignited to signal to aerial assets such as helicopter gunships the direction of the enemy approach. It is most often used as a last resort for passing enemy attack vector information when radio communication between the compound defenders and the gunship pilots becomes disrupted.

The morning of July 23 finally arrived. One day and a wake-up to go. It was time to head to MACV in Sài Gòn to begin out-processing. As

I made the rounds offering my goodbyes, I was strongly conflicted. Of course, I wanted to go home. I could not wait to get home. But I was leaving a job unfinished and separating myself from men who had become close friends, indeed brothers, leaving them to complete the battle without me.

My last stop in saying goodbye was the district chief. We had a mutually respectful relationship almost from the beginning of my tour. As I entered his office, I saw him alone, sitting at his desk. I walked up to him, stood at attention, saluted, and told him in Vietnamese that I had finished my time in Việt Nam.

I avoided formality. But this one time would be the only time in Việt Nam I would, of conscious volition, show such respectful formality to a superior officer, American or Vietnamese. He stared at me stoically, or so he tried, but a flash of sorrow at my departure showed through. I turned on my heel, walked out, and got into the waiting jeep, ready to head out. I am not usually an emotional person, but the conflicting feelings were starting to get to me. "Get me out of here," I told the driver with a catch in my throat. It was a terribly sad feeling. The driver of the M151 jeep released the hand brake, turned the wheel, and we splashed through the monsoon season puddles in the reddish earth making our way to, then through, the front gate. The war, for me, was over. Or so I thought.

About two hours later, I arrived at MACV out-processing in Sài Gòn. I would be there until wheels up two days hence, on the 25th of July. As I walked into the barracks to select a bunk for my brief stay, I overheard murmuring and grumbling. I saw some other lieutenants eyeballing, apparently upset about me, a military intelligence officer, wearing a Combat Infantry Badge cloth patch on my jungle fatigue uniform. The Army had awarded me the CIB because I held an infantry slot and I had come under fire and fought back. I had been told it was exceedingly difficult for an intelligence officer to receive this award and that it had required a corps-level waiver. Major Barnett and at least one senior officer at province headquarters had pushed for it. It was awarded for action against the enemy, and I was proud to be among their number.

Emotions were sometimes magnified in Việt Nam, and that was true at the MACV out-processing facility. The men's restroom stalls had some of the most hilarious graffiti I had seen—truly creative wordsmiths had been at work. Interestingly, two years after I returned to the World, an issue of *Playboy* featured a story on precisely that latrine graffiti.

Finally, DEROS (Date of Estimated Return from Overseas Service) day arrived. After breakfast, I pulled out my dress khakis, preparing to put them on before making the short bus ride to Tân Sơn Nhứt airport. I hung my uniform on the locker door, appropriately decorated with the ribbons and CIB I had earned, including the Purple Heart. The number of medals did not go unnoticed by the grumbling lieutenants, whose attitude turned to respectful nods and acknowledgements. It was a feeling of satisfaction, at the conclusion of my wartime effort, to be appreciated by my peers for the work we undertook.

The freedom bird was full and, as many on flights before mine have reported, a cheer went up from the men when we lifted off the ground. My time in Việt Nam was over, and I had strongly conflicting feelings about it. The return trip on the chartered flight took us through Japan and Anchorage, Alaska, finally ending at Travis Air Force Base. I shared the one-hour ride to San Francisco International Airport with another officer I met on the return flight.

I had a few hours' layover at the airport, but time did not drag too much. I was soon aboard a Delta Airlines jet with almost no one on the plane. I had the good fortune to get a stewardess, as they were called in 1970, who had a brother in Việt Nam. She could not do enough for me. The flight was of further interest because another soldier, a new second lieutenant, was leaving his hometown for an assignment in Washington, DC. I tried to explain to this fellow lieutenant that there was no actual rank between us. Second or first lieutenant did not matter in how we addressed each other. There was no *Sir-ing* involved. But this impressionable officer insisted on showing respect, probably because of the fruit salad, or medals I wore. Okay, as I relaxed into the last leg of my journey home, I can live with that.

There were many eyes on me, walking the gangway to the arrival terminal. Việt Nam was still a big news item, and while not all the public put blame for US participation in the war on the soldiers, many did. And it would be another generation of American societal maturity before the shame of that action would be realized in the hearts of most Americans.

As I was an unmarried man without a girlfriend, my parents were there to give me a ride back home. It was a disjointed feeling. My father's particularly embracing hug, most unlike him, was reassuring that I had made it back. But I felt incongruous and out of place in this land free from war, where everyday people were not so concerned about personal safety.

An hour later, I was home, and things looked familiar and yet not. My folks wanted to talk to me further, but I needed sleep. I turned in and slept for more than twelve hours. I woke thinking my life had been permanently changed, as had I, and would require an extended period of readjustment.

PART THREE

The Consequences

Chapter 20
Things Get Dicey

A rriving home at my parents' house was a minor event—the requisite welcoming sign in the yard for the neighbors to see. "Loewer Power," it said. Well, okay. À propos for my family and blue-collar community of my roots. And yes, "Loewer" rhymes with "Power." But I felt as if perhaps I had outgrown this kind of celebration. It was strange coming back to the World. I did not seem to fit. Everyone appeared concerned, indeed driven, by things that were not important to me. Life and death conflict had been replaced with neighborhood goings-on.

Once I crossed the threshold of my boyhood home, I did not venture out for three weeks. I did not tell anyone I was home during what became a decompression period. But eventually, like so many combat vets, I seemed to adjust to the pre-military routine. At least superficially. My view of the world was different now. And I had trouble understanding why people could not see the important things in life. They were focused on trivial matters.

I recall an occasion when I had been home two weeks. Unknown to me, my mom had committed me to help drive a neighbor to a doctor's appointment, a seemingly reasonable thing to do. But when she told me of this task, I became upset. It angered me suddenly and deeply. I glared at her intently and told her, "Do not ever do something like that again." The look on her face showed how scared she was at my reaction. I surprised myself at how strongly I had responded. I think it was because she had committed me to a mundane task without my consent, while I knew that I was *not* helping my combat brothers whom I had left behind just fifteen days ago.

A week later, I drove sixty miles south to Alexandria, Virginia, to get an apartment at my next duty assignment—the 902nd Military Intelligence Group located there. The 902nd was considered *the* elite MI group. Unlike the other CONUS MI groups, the 902nd was wire-charted directly under ACSI—the assistant chief of staff for Intelligence at the Pentagon. I had requested this assignment because I wanted to take University of Maryland night classes at the Pentagon to complete my bachelor's degree mathematics program requirements. Fortunately, the powers that be could accommodate the assignment preference of men returning from Viêt Nam.

I reported to the 902nd in civilian clothes, standard dress for my 9666 MOS. Within two months, they sent me to New York City as a dignitary bodyguard for the United Nations celebration of their twenty-fifth anniversary—operation UN25. I was one of a team of four agents coming north from Virginia, and they put us up in a moderately comfortable hotel. We were assigned to guard some of the attending diplomats. I drew Golda Meir, prime minister of Israel; Ferdinand Marcos, president of the Philippines; and Secretary of State William P. Rogers. It was mostly boring work but kind of fun to legally conceal-carry a .38-Special on the subways of New York.

I met another intelligence agent, Dan, from Philadelphia, in the course of my duties. Dan was recently back from Viêt Nam as well, and I got along exceedingly well with him. I liked his relaxed and amiable manner, comfortable to be around. He seemed to enjoy my company too. So, while neither of us were given to drink much alcohol, we decided a visit to a New York bar was a must-do while in the Big Apple. At the end of our shift, we left the hotel, walked a few blocks down 42nd Street, entered the establishment, and took seats at the bar.

Neither Dan nor I had any experience carrying a concealed handgun in the United States. Wearing these .38-Special revolvers under our sports coats was something we were still getting used to. They must have projected out under our coats as we leaned on the stools toward the bar and our drinks. The bartender suggested, "Anybody want to check their guns at the bar?" We laughed, but as my Mai Tai was being mixed, Dan studied my expression, paused and nodded at the back bar, and deadpanned, "Do you know what I want to do?" I looked straight ahead and saw a line of holiday pumpkins reflecting from the bottom of the mirror. "Does it have anything to do with those pumpkins?" I went along. He smiled, responding to the crazy common interest of shooting up the pumpkins.

Dan and I bonded quickly. As we talked, we shared our wartime and stateside history. Later in the evening, he tried to interest me in joining an organized crime task force that was being put together in Philly. While the prospect of that kind of an opportunity got my attention, my plans to complete the degree program in mathematics were incompatible with it and the relo it would entail. And certainly, my soon-to-emerge psych problems would have been a showstopper. Nonetheless, I told Dan I would think about it. A few weeks after returning home, he called me, and I officially gave it a pass.

Among the tasking opportunities available at the 902nd was joining one of the Survey Teams, groups of four men who travelled nationally to inspect high-security installations in various parts of the country. I opted in and was assigned to the Pacific team, which meant we were going to Hawaii. I was thrilled with the prospect.

On the stunningly beautiful island of Oahu, I enjoyed the thirty days of evening teriyaki steak at the Pieces of Eight restaurant on Lewers Street in downtown Waikiki, with its life-sized Jolly Roger statue, and piano playing by Grant. Our accommodations were at the Coral Reef hotel.

We were wrapping up our inspection and had gathered in a small conference room at the secure facility to brief an officer senior staff of about thirty men. Another team member began iterating through his findings when a senior officer assigned there interrupted to ask a question. The team member hesitated to respond, so I picked up the ball and started to run with it. I got out only ten words and my mind went completely blank. I suddenly felt anxious and cold. The loss was beyond embarrassing. I could no longer speak. My mind was completely fogged in and I could not continue. Fortunately, another senior officer from the staff pivoted on the topic and the conversation went on along a new line of discussion.

It was six months to the day from my return from Viêt Nam. While combat nightmares and insomnia were part of my life, I did not connect my service in Viêt Nam to the incident. But decades later, this unfortunate aphasic event would prove to be the beginning of my professional undoing from combat PTSD.

I had let the team down, embarrassed them in the worst way. I pulled the team leader aside that evening and requested a transfer from this survey team job to a position with the Pentagon Counter-intelligence Force (PCF), part of the 902nd at the Pentagon. The next survey team assignment would not be for a few months, so there was plenty of time to arrange the transfer. Further, by putting the request in myself, the 902nd would realize I was more than okay with it.

In the interim, an open and helpful field grade officer, Major Richard Black, suggested to me I consider the army's Bootstrap program a year after I made captain. Under the terms of this opportunity, I could go back to college and complete my degree requirements, drawing full military pay and allowances, and not have to report in for a period of up to two years. Dick Black pointed out that if I took such a course of action, when my degree program was completed, I would "be looking the majority in the face." He meant, of course, I would have enough time in grade as a captain to be nearly eligible for promotion to the rank of major. It meant a career in the military. Although my combat assignment achievement had left me well-positioned for advancement, to make such a choice would have been unwise. The anxiety attacks would badly short-circuit this plan. I decided to transfer to PCF, take evening classes, and leave the military after another year.

The transfer and job with PCF went well. Working at the Pentagon made possible my evening classes there, as I earned credits toward the completion of my bachelor's degree. But it also was a challenge. The branch I commanded oversaw Pentagon premises security as it applied to classified documents. I had forty-five men working for me, seeking evidence of security violations throughout the Pentagon. Morale, however, among the young men in the branch was exceptionally low. Apparently, some men had been pranking the previous branch commander and, as a result, trust had completely broken down. Attempts at retribution between the branch CO and his men were commonplace. It was time for a change and an undertaking I intended to do. But problems lay ahead. The work was mundane and uninspired. The evening shift for most of the men was flat-out boring—checking offices for classified documents left out in the open. I was determined to improve security on all shifts by spicing things up.

I initiated ad hoc penetration inspections. We would try to enter by pretext various high-security installations within the Pentagon. Two of the more memorable penetration successes come to mind. The

Joint Chiefs of Staff (JCS) had sections of the Pentagon where entry was controlled by guards. Bypassing security required mounting an adequate ploy to fool the guard on duty. We did not have JCS badges, so we had to exhibit some other reason of appearing to belong there.

It was not difficult at all, although their security no doubt has improved since those days. We wore workmen's clothing, put on tool belts, grabbed a ladder that was setting out near a maintenance crew, toted some surplus thick telephone wire and handsets, and walked through the gate when the guard was busy. We had no nefarious intent; we were only proving the point that the guards could be lax in admitting personnel. After penetrating the facility, we went to the security office and told them how we gained entry. No muss, no fuss. They got the benefit of learning where they needed to beef up security, and my men got firsthand experience in ad hoc penetration inspections.

The second notable penetration we achieved was the Pentagon Telecommunications Center (PTC). We frequently entered facilities by crawling above the dropped ceiling tiles. In this case, we found a large hole in the perimeter wall where workmen had run through many pipes of conduit. The problem for the PTC was the workmen had not filled in the wall space around the conduit after they had run it.

The open space in the wall encircling the conduit was minimal, but large enough for a person to squeeze through. We entered and walked above the ceiling, listening to the conversations below. I advanced about fifty feet to a small storage area beneath us, removed a two-by-four-foot ceiling tile, and dropped to the top of an unlocked Mosler safe holding highly classified documents.

I exited the storage room into a hallway and presented my badge and credentials to the first person I encountered. The middle-aged woman was surprised and then appeared shocked when I told her to report to her security officer and bring him here. The security officer, a serious and portly man, listened intently as I again presented my Bs and Cs, and began explaining who we were and how we had gained entry. He appeared especially concerned, as I had hoped he would.

To his credit, he listened carefully and like me, had only the focus of fixing the problem. Here, that meant repairing the hole in the wall above the ceiling tiles through which we had gained entry. I explained to him I would not file any paper on this; my thrust was only to alert him of the weakness in their security and provide an impetus to get it repaired. His response was satisfyingly direct: "It will get fixed immediately." We left the facility through the front door and headed out to lunch. It was not a bad morning's work.

The next day I returned, entered the area above the PTC where the conduit was put through the wall, and saw that they had secured it. The workmen had completely covered the exposed area. My guess was the security officer was probably going to add a mechanism, such as ultrasonic sensors, to detect movement above the ceiling. That would have been completely his call, but it was what I would have done.

I considered the ad hoc penetration inspections an effective tool to tighten installation security in the Pentagon. It was also a well-appreciated diversion for the men. There were a few other examples of offices we penetrated and how we managed it, but they are best not publicly discussed. I will say that I appreciated the latitude of my commanding officer, Lieutenant Colonel Richard Hawes, and my immediate supervisor, Major Robert Loomis, in allowing me to use these atypical methods of boosting Pentagon security. The public probably did not realize that in the early 1970s, there were over thirty-five hostile foreign intelligence agencies operating in the Washington, DC area, and that the Pentagon building was open to the public. It was a much bigger problem than people knew.

Another issue we dealt with were bomb threats. During my time at the Pentagon, we did not encounter any actual bombs, only threats that sometimes involved bomb-appearing devices workmen had left behind after completion of an office build-out job. A major threat to our work in cordoning off the area and preserving the scene was, unbelievably, senior military officers. On more than one occasion, senior officers would try to use their rank to bring an impressionable secretary or two to the site to personally "just take a quick look" of the apparent bomb. If what I saw was any sign, the secretary was gaining a thrill by accompanying the officer as he wielded power, something the officer presumably would try to cash in on later.

I saw only one way to deter this stupidity, and it was effective. I asked the men responding with me to bring our portable videotaping equipment. I would explain to the gawking brass that I needed their images on tape for body identification purposes, should the bomb explode. That was usually enough to dull the secretary's interest and convince the field grade officer to do the discretion-is-a-better-part-of-valor thing and return to his office.

My attitude on a career for others in the military was neutral. While I was sympathetic to the anti-war movement, I held the strong view that protestors must operate within the laws of our country. Dissent is a vital part of our heritage and our constitution, and both sides, the protestors and the establishment, must respect it.

My evening classes toward my B.S. in mathematics were progressing, and I intended to return to the University of Maryland at College Park full-time. Anxiety was running high 24/7, and I compensated by drinking Mai Tais at restaurants. I was not much of an alcohol consumer, however. I did not care for the taste of it, but it enabled me to get through the minimal number of social situations I would agree to attending.

By this time, they had promoted me to the rank of captain. It was more or less an automatic action from one year in grade as a first lieutenant. But captain or not, I identified with the enlisted soldiers, the ranks from where I came. I grew my hair long, and from time to time, was admonished for it. I recall a time Lieutenant Colonel Hawes, a fine gentleman and officer whom I respected, called me into his office after I had applied for release from active duty. He told me two things. First, he scolded, "Get a haircut." Second, he wanted me to reconsider leaving the Army. He suggested I stay in because he believed I was "open and honest and identified with the common soldier." Well, I valued his opinion and told him I would think about what he suggested. I did, but only briefly. An objection I had with staying in was, while I saw many competent officers in the Army, I saw some whose competence in Viêt Nam was easily questionable. I frankly did not like seeing how that incompetence could and did get people killed.

And while I still thought of Viêt Nam a lot, I had become pacified. I had no interest in weapons or the killing of any creatures. I no longer wanted to go fishing; I saw it as cruel. I had come to believe the weaker living things among us should be protected, or at least not casually killed. I had a new perspective now. I saw the minority point of view. Although my fellow man by and large found humor in my opinion and actions, I knew most of them were in no position to judge me on this issue. They neither had nor could understand my experiences.

The one bright light during this tough time was when I met my wife. A friend and fellow worker at the 902nd, First Lieutenant Perry Polinsky went with me to a men's clothing store, Bonds, at the Landmark shopping mall in Alexandria. I needed an extra shirt rather badly. Perry waited outside the store while I entered and was met by an alluring woman, Terrie, who wanted to wait on me. I liked her at

My wife, Terrie, and I sitting on a small island in the Potomac
River by Fletcher's Boat House in the summer of 1971.
Photo by my good friend, Lieutenant Paul Simms.

first sight and ended up buying the shirt. I also purchased cuff links, a couple of ties, and a belt. Well, I suppose I liked her a great deal. As I left the store and Perry and I headed for the car, I mentioned I had bought more than I'd intended and why. He commented, "Did you ask her out?" "No," I replied. He gave me a *you dumbass* kind of dismissive look, so I walked back into the store and made the date. We have been together ever since. I lost touch with Perry after leaving the military, but each year on our anniversary, Terrie and I fondly remember Perry Polinsky.

One of the evening classes I took at the Pentagon was taught by a forty-something Middle Eastern professor, Dr. "Mary." It was a typical entry-level Government and Politics class that many bachelor's degree candidates selected to fulfill part of the general education requirement. Since we had a small class of perhaps twenty students, Mary preferred that this after-hours group sit around the enormous conference table in a borrowed Pentagon office. I liked this relaxed gathering. It was more of a seminar than a lecture, conducive to discussion.

We debated general G & P topics and those in the news. Mary treated us as peers, making the discussion open and easy for the students to contribute. But as the weeks went by, the instructor drilled down on biographical data from the students. She was particularly interested in rank and positions of them, all of whom worked at the Pentagon. The detail she sought in her questions raised an eyebrow. It seemed to be more than one would expect in get-acquainted chatting.

The following day, I made a trip to headquarters and talked to a few people to see if Mary was on their radar. The 902nd had counterintelligence responsibility for the Pentagon but this situation was beyond what the agents at PCF were aware of.

I was informed they knew her. Mary openly identified her birthplace as Turkey, but they believed her to have been born in the Soviet Union close to the Turkish border. They considered her a likely *spotter* for the KGB. A spotter, in this context, is someone who locates people who have access to classified information and may be suitable targets for recruitment as spies. Once identified, Soviet agents would step in and assess the target's vulnerabilities and motivations. While teaching her class on government and politics, Mary would perform as a Soviet spotter, continuing to elicit information from Pentagon workers and passing it up her chain of command. That was the Intelligence Community's assessment of Mary.

Since I was a counterintelligence agent on duty in the Pentagon, I almost never wore my uniform. All people "knew" about me was I was yet another civilian, documented as a GS-11, working somewhere in the bowels of that building. One evening in her class, Mary called on me to contribute my thoughts to the topic on the table. After I answered her question, she asked where I worked and the nature of my job. I rebuffed her questioning, which threw her off, but she came back and asked if I were military or not. This was getting uncomfortable, and I needed to end it, so I represented myself as my documentation indicated. She stopped her questioning. Whether she knew my actual rank, captain, and job as counterintelligence agent, I do not know. But we finished the semester with no further personal interest in me from either Mary or a new acquaintance interested in getting to know me.

It was nearing my REFRAD date of December 20, 1971, and my time in the Army was winding down. Someone at headquarters thought it was appropriate to have me address the entire 902nd MI Group on the subject of the new Modern Volunteer Army initiative. Yes, this guy who could not speak in front of a small group of fellow officers was to present to an auditorium of several hundred men and women. Needless to say, my anxiety was extremely high. And I did not understand why. After all, while I was nervous presenting in high school six years earlier, I acted in school plays each year there, once in a lead role. Calling me shy was a fair statement. But why such tremendous anxiety? Why the symptoms, always the same: hyperarousal, heart racing, a cold sensation over my body, sweaty hands that stuck to paper I handled, mental fog rolling in such that I could not easily choose the correct word, and losing the thread of thought of the subject I was talking about.

The date of my talk arrived too soon. In setting up my plan for the presentation, I finessed my time on stage by showing a film—General William Westmoreland on the Modern Volunteer Army. It was à propos because it was topical, and I would introduce the virtual "him" and emphasize the importance of working within the system. I admonished the men who worked for me ahead of time not to ask me questions. I did not need the further difficulty or embarrassment.

Unexpectedly, the new commander of the 902nd, who had arrived from his last duty station, came in and sat in the front row. This was going to be a disaster. In preparation, I wrote out my brief introductory remarks, word for word, and when introduced, I walked to the podium and delivered the intro to the film. My tongue was not working, it seemed, and the message for the troops barely was delivered. I finished and walked uncomfortably off the stage, followed by developing audience murmurs. Perhaps if I had worn my uniform providing some context, they would have been more understanding. But that was wishful thinking. Even so, few military intelligence men had my depth of combat experience. The instant respect such medals produce might have softened the situation.

I had no idea of the relationship between this anxiety attack and the attack on the CRIP operation of February 25, 1970 that killed my friend, Recon platoon leader Jeff Riek and his RTO, Bob Mossgrove. It would be decades before I made the link to my survivor guilt, being pulled from that operation at the last minute to brief a visiting dignitary.

Other trauma manifestations appeared. I resisted going out in public and did not want to eat anywhere but at home. On one occasion, while I was dating Terrie, I took her for a quick bite to a local McDonald's. On the way there I had an anxiety attack—heart racing, a cold sensation over my body, severe hand tremor, brain fog, and aphasic speech pattern emerging. I had recently started dating Terrie and was afraid this odd and crippling behavior pattern would scare her away. But she remained unfazed and developed an understanding, perhaps well before I did, of how war can affect people. As we approached McDonald's, it became too intense for me. I drove through the drive-in lane, ordered, picked up our food, and then pulled into a parking space, where we ate. Even with this accommodation, I could not pick up a cup without its contents spilling. The feeling of helplessness was overpowering, being reduced to this, but there was nothing I could do. It was an emasculating experience.

These behaviors were the beginning of the manifestation of combat Post-Traumatic Stress Disorder, initially several months after my return from Viêt Nam, and then a year later, entrenched and almost totally socially disabling. The 902nd briefing had forced me into an untenable situation, one that psychologically mirrored the circumstances of Jeff's death. It was the operation I was scheduled to take and was pulled from, the operation whose intelligence was provided by me. The one I was not on because of a fucking briefing.

Regarding this operation on that day in February, I cannot help but think had I gone, I, too, might have been a casualty. Frequently on CRIP ops, the Recon platoon leader and I, in sync with our respective RTOs, would stand together, reviewing aspects of the operation. The enemy had chosen to kill, in their surprise volley, the senior-most American and his means of communication. That I was pulled out of this operation to brief—to present to a group of people—was both a blessing and a condemnation. It was fortunate because it probably spared my life. But distressing because Jeff's and Bob's deaths were too close to me. I felt responsible and guilty about it for several reasons: I sent the intelligence down of the possible enemy activity, I was pulled from the operation and avoided sharing the risk, and I survived. Jeff, a West Point officer and son of a proud military family, the guy who wanted to join me on R&R in Australia, was now dead.

The 20th of December 1971 arrived, and I found myself ambivalent to the events. It was time to move on, to get back to the world of academia I anticipated with more than mild interest. But it was also time to say goodbye to the men I served with, and to all things military, including Việt Nam. And with that intention, how little I understood myself and the mental bogeyman my mind had now unwittingly embraced. The psych problem was just beginning.

I had written to the Vietnamese Intel squad through my former interpreter a couple of times since returning home and even investigated and received permission to go back to Tân Trụ for a visit. But deep down, I knew it was all up to them now. Before my tour in Việt Nam was completed, the Americans had begun to pull out. Everyone understood where it was headed. The Vietnamese would soon be on their own, and I hoped to God they could handle it. I worried that while most of the riceroots people were nationalistic, too many of them had quietly retained their antipathy toward the corrupt Sài Gòn government and even sympathies for the Việt Cộng. Some of the strictly nationalistic might easily align with the enemy should the tide turn away from the GVN. In any case, there was nothing left for me except concern for the brothers who would see it through to the last, whatever the outcome. Deep regret, as unlikely as it might seem, was felt for the Vietnamese, who had no choice but to remain behind.

Chapter 21

You Are on Your Own, Kid

In the spring of 1972, it was satisfying to get back to campus full-time. The last I was there in that capacity was the fall of 1967, my final semester before dropping out and signing up for time with Uncle Sam. My class schedule was heavy with early math for math majors, and on a lark, I opted for an uncredited computer workshop supporting differential calculus. The computer was a UNIVAC 1108, a multi-CPU mainframe that allowed less than one hundred concurrent users. It was more than enough, though, to grab me by the stacking swivel, and I never looked back. I switched my major from math to General Physical Sciences, the closest thing they had to a computer science baccalaureate degree program. While I performed well in my courses, I found that using slide rule scales and completing tasks had both become much more difficult. To assist me in calculations, I bought an HP-35 scientific calculator, the world's first with trigonometric and exponential functions. It cost a whopping $395.00 in 1972 but was well worth it to me.

In the summer of 1974, I graduated from the University of Maryland with a B.S. degree. Unknown to me, I had coincidentally completed the requirements for the newly established Computer Science baccalaureate degree. At the suggestion of Professor Vic Basili, I accepted that choice and became the first student at U of M to earn the degree in computer science.

Along the way, I reluctantly accepted that my intense anxiety when speaking in public was a permanent affliction. I did not understand why. And its exacerbation continued. I was uncomfortable—I felt unsafe—going out in public. But while the anxiety greatly restricted my ability to openly converse in the classroom setting, my love for computers was intense and I had little difficulty conversing with them.

I married my two-year sweetheart, Terrie, in 1972, and in doing so, made her a computer widow. I would disappear from our apartment in Greenbelt, Maryland, to the new computer sciences building on campus in College Park at all hours, and for unspecified periods of time. I used the GI bill to pay for school, and Terrie worked as the manager at Famous Maid, a junior shop at a local strip mall to pay our living expenses. But by the autumn of 1974, all was forgiven. I cashed in on our hard work for my first non-military professional job as a computer programmer at the Defense Intelligence Agency (DIA) at Arlington Hall Station in Arlington, Virginia.

Life at DIA was not uncommonly different from other government agencies. There was a written procedure for doing nearly everything, and innovation was resisted as a matter of course. The public speaking problem became more acute as I had great difficultly even talking to my coworkers at, for example, a five-person section meeting. I recall jumping out of my seat, on one occasion, as a meeting was beginning. The anxiety was suddenly overwhelming. I felt a fight-or-flight response. I hurried to the men's room, splashed water on my face, and stared into the mirror. Looking at me was a red, gob smacked, dripping wet visage. I asked myself, *What the hell is happening?* It was a PTSD attack, one that I did not understand. I returned to the meeting and limped through participation with the help of my coworkers, who knew I was a combat veteran, and perhaps suspected its root cause more accurately than I. But this was unnerving, and I realized I had to learn to hide or avoid provoking these symptoms as best I could if I were to have any kind of professional life.

At home, I had to keep busy. We had our first child, Sarah, and the second, Wendy, was on the way. Space was limited in our two-bedroom cottage in old Falls Church, Virginia, so I built a set of bunk beds anticipating the need. I found solace in projects like this, so I stepped up and added an eight-by-twelve-foot back porch to the house, an especially useful upgrade for an emerging family. While the projects kept me busy after the workday and on weekends, gaining restful sleep continued to be problematic. We bought a king-sized bed to help protect my pregnant wife from my sleeping fits, periods during the night where I would suddenly and violently kick out at whatever was close. Terrie would wake me from the combat nightmares, but only after suffering bruises from the attacks.

During my third year at DIA, I competed for and won an opportunity to go to graduate school for a year at full salary. I enrolled as a Master of Computer Science candidate but knew I would never complete the program. As it was structured then, the program required an oral examination as a thesis defense for the degree. I was still ill-equipped to discuss even informal topics in most settings. I thought about talking to my faculty advisor regarding an accommodation for the future oral exam, but my problem did not fit into any offered category. How could I explain it to the advisor when I did not understand it myself? And the embarrassment was more than I wanted to go through.

The university time went by quickly, and I added more credits toward my master's degree in computer science. But I had nearly topped out with my government GS rating for technical non-management, leaving me with little maneuvering room for advancement at DIA. So, it was time to make a change.

On the advice of a former DIA coworker, I went to work for Telenet Communications Corporation, a seventy-five-man organization on 15th Street in Washington, DC. Telenet, established by Bolt, Beranek, and Newman, Inc., had developed and was selling packet-switched networks using the X.25 wide area network protocol. The president of the company, Larry Roberts, was the former head of ARPANET. At Telenet, they gave me responsibility for maintenance and enhancement of the protocol layer of the X.25 software. The pre-Internet public packet-switching technology was drawing serious clients, given the reduced cost for long-distance communications on the microprocessor-based network nodes. However, as with any emerging technology that promised a lower cost of business, customers insisted on equal or better product reliability.

> A packet-switched network is a communications network that "packetizes" messages into smaller piece messages and sends them across the network to their destination. The packets may go different routes on the network to arrive at the endpoint, where they are reassembled into the original message. Communications from many different customers can be transmitted this way, sharing the network, and thus reducing the transmission costs.

One such organization, TRW, moved its point of sale credit card devices to the network and at first enjoyed success. It was not long before a problem developed, however, as traffic increased on the microprocessor-driven nodes. "Karl," my immediate supervisor, explained that the company's credit card transactions were suddenly disconnecting before the charge could be completed.

TRW was threatening to terminate the contract, and soon. A fix was needed *now*. It was a troubleshooter opportunity, and it piqued my interest. The pressure was on! I saw it as my charge;

a high-risk opportunity to pull a rabbit out of a hat and doing it independently of coworkers. I knew I did my best work when my back was against the wall.

I spent about an hour intensely reviewing the handshaking code in the protocol connection establishment phase and found what I believed to be a hole in the software logic. I explained my thinking to Karl, who immediately picked up on it. He modified the code correcting the problem and incrementing a counter if the pathological "connection collision" condition occurred. As I walked by a coworker, Ben, a few hours later, he remarked, "You don't waste any time, do you?" We put the debugger on the packet switch memory and sure enough, the pathological collision condition was detected and had been obviated by the correction to the code.

The software modification was easy to do, and TRW became a satisfied and continuing customer. Being called in to troubleshoot a software problem had a special appeal to me. Intensely focusing on a single problem allowed me to work independently from others and kept me away from meetings. An answer to a prayer, I thought. I should troubleshoot for a living. A quick in. Solve the problem. A quick out.

But in truth, it spoke to a more deeply held need: the necessity to control what was happening, perhaps subconsciously, to avoid a reoccurrence of some of the horror of Viêt Nam when the decisions were not my own. The compulsion to be in charge rather than one of the flock, going along with whatever another may decide. Not unlike a John Milton characterization: *Better to reign in Hell than serve in Heaven.*

Karl and I had a positive relationship, but the anxiety issues associated with typical work responsibilities were increasing in severity and driving me into a longer-term state of lethargy. I could see that I was withdrawing from life, but I could not overcome it. The situation came to a head one afternoon when Karl asked me to give a brief talk to my coworkers. I agonized over it for several days, then went to his office to tell him I could not do it, and that I was prepared to resign my position if he thought that an appropriate thing to do.

I explained to him I was not comfortable speaking before a group, hoping that would be enough of a reason. He was not pleased with what I said and barked "That is no excuse!" I felt a rush of anger. "I was not offering an excuse. I was giving you an explanation," I countered. He stopped and got a more serious and reflective look on his face. I walked to the window in his office, stared out and said, "I have a problem speaking to groups of people. Before Việt Nam, there was no problem." I did not know for certain that the severe anxiety was connected to my wartime service, but no other life events fit that accounting. Karl appeared to understand even more than I was saying, and directly expressed, "You will not have to do that while you work here." Then he repeated what he had said to reinforce the point. Perhaps his view was borne from experiences in his mother country—Germany. Karl grasped the personal impact of the problem, and I was relieved and grateful.

But deep down, the incident had left me feeling less than comfortable in this situation, believing that it could arise again in this growing organization. I began to think seriously of setting up my own company where I could control the degree of public contact.

In 1977, the world of computers was beginning to benefit from the microprocessor. Retail stores were opening to sell the likes of Altair, North Star, and Cromemco equipment for personal and business computing.

I talked to my brother-in-law, Chuck Rieger, a PhD from Stanford, and a professor of artificial intelligence in the Computer Science department at the University of Maryland. I asked if he knew of

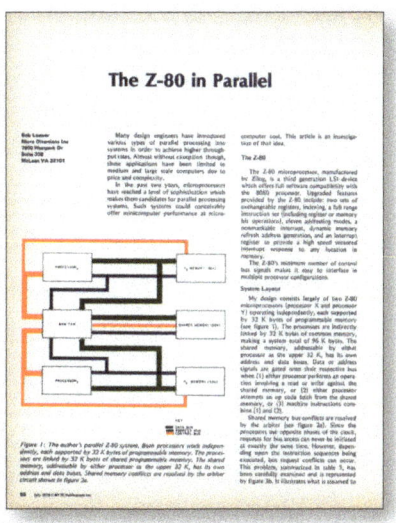

anyone who might be open to partnering in a computer business, aimed at capitalizing on the microprocessor revolution. His response was that *he* was interested. I was pleased, and we began our collaboration developing, manufacturing, and selling advanced video hardware for the S100 bus, and later, IBM personal computer markets. Chuck, a pensive and brilliant man whose intellectual curiosity was infinite, had been my advisor at U of M. He had gone out of his way more than once to help me wrap up my baccalaureate program in computer science as my social integration difficulties intensified.

One of my research topics at the university was the Zilog Z-80 microprocessor and its advanced instruction set. I toyed with ways to run this processor in parallel using shared memory and put together a design for it. I drafted an article about it, "The Z-80 in Parallel," submitted it to *BYTE* magazine (bought by McGraw-Hill) and they printed it. Great—age thirty-one, only a bachelor's degree, and I was published.

My partnership with Chuck continued for eight years. We staffed up, bringing onboard Craig Denbrook, an ace hardware/software man

I knew from my days at the DIA; Brad Mandell, an operating systems Air Force major I also knew from DIA; Jim Mather, a marketing and sales contemporary from Baltimore's Dundalk Senior High class of 1965; and Tom Skillman, an impressive student of Chuck's.

The most popular of Chuck's creations was Microangelo, a raster graphics S100 bus printed circuit single-board computer capable of displaying 480 x 512-pixel graphics. It was quite advanced for its time and had many buyers, particularly in academic and government research circles.

Photo courtesy Scion Corporation

While Chuck ran the technical department, and conceptualized and developed our products, I oversaw administration, manufacturing, and sales. I liked my job, getting my hands in many departments, learning new things. I moved my family from Falls Church to Reston and added a back porch to our new house—I was getting good at this—but the distraction was not enough to help me psychologically. Social interactions were nearly nonexistent. The few times I could take the family out to eat were a stilted scene. I would race through the meal, and insist on leaving when I finished, often departing before my family could complete their meals.

Micro Diversions, Inc. products were well ahead of their time. Chuck's manifested imagination brought us big-league attention in multiple serious financing opportunities. But as a company, we were a collection of entrepreneurs, not corporate executives, or *maintenance men* as I used to jokingly call them. We clung to parochial attitudes about letting go any of the company stock that might wrest control away from us. Too much sweat and sacrifice had gone into growing the company from the ground up to about $1.5 million in annual sales. Looking back on it years later, however, I saw the failing to prudently respond to the funding initiatives as an example of how my personal limitations, to a degree, could work against the company's interests.

Over that year, we had significant investment interest from four sources: Telenet, my former employer, had several senior executives investigate the worth and fit of our products to theirs; Timeplex, Inc. visited us, their CEO expressing a direct interest in buying the company; a deep pocket in Texas, a friend of Congressman Charlie Rose with whom we had a special relationship, was a candidate for investment; and a pair of venture capitalists wanting to be onboard "as the train was leaving the station."

But nearly to a man, we addressed these opportunities with more apprehension than appreciation, leaning toward finishing the journey from bootstraps to a solid balance sheet on our own. We collectively breathed the spirit of Nietzsche when he proclaimed, "Nothing ever succeeds which exuberant spirits have not helped to produce." Nonetheless, the company eventually closed on first stage financing with the venture group out of necessity to fund growth.

As the company and the need to interface with more prominent people grew, psych issues became an even greater difficulty for me. When I knew I could no longer be capable in my job as CEO and was in effect holding back the company's opportunities, I stepped down and stepped out. The move gave the company more maneuvering room and competence at the top, and gave me what

I needed most, a place to work where I could more fully control the public interfacing. I birthed another company to capitalize on a full text searching algorithm I had read about and for which I had enhancement ideas.

I modified the full text algorithm in a way to improve its effectiveness in very high-speed pattern matching applications of unstructured data and to dramatically reduce its system load. This established clear, market noticeable differences from its search system competition architecture known as *inverted file*. I asked David Stoffel, an enterprising young man blinded as a teenager by disease, to program a software prototype based on the new algorithm. The implementation was an impressive enough demonstration to complete the negotiation of the sale of forty-seven percent of the start-up company for $1.5 million.

The seed financing was a huge success. But more importantly, forming the new company permitted me to hire an experienced CEO to run it and get back to the world of software development. This was one that allowed me control of my work, instead of the time I otherwise would have had to spend dealing with the anxiety from interfacing with people.

Chapter 22

Making Sense of It

It was a few years after it opened before I made my first visit to the Việt Nam Veterans Memorial. It appeared different to me then than it does today, early on that Saturday morning, fog rising off the Potomac. Surprisingly, I had found a parking space in West Potomac Park. I was alone but on a mission as I made my way on foot north toward the Wall. I moved slowly most of the way, past the Lincoln Memorial and the Reflecting Pool, when a family of four hurried by. My inward thoughts were interrupted by the pre-teen among them, lamenting her required participation in the visit. "Why should I have to go to a memorial set up by the same guys it is for?" Well, it was unfortunate to hear that. Her young mind had missed the point entirely.

The Wall was erected by the combat survivors of the Việt Nam War because their country had no interest in recognizing the contribution of their dead brothers. The lack of interest was because the war had not ended with a clear victory. The American people's reaction to Việt Nam combat veterans was a national shame that would go unrealized for another generation or more. I was one of those survivors and had friends' identities recorded here, the men who did not make it home, the men who made the ultimate sacrifice.

I had conflicting thoughts about this visit to the Wall. I was not sure I could complete it. This was a sacred place to many of us. But

211

establishing a monument to these brave men seemed both *entirely fitting* and, yet, not quite right. It was a sense of trepidation and foreboding I felt, something anticipated, yet I was not sure anything was to happen.

I approached from the south, through a line of trees opposing and parallel to the Wall. I stooped over in the tree line, feeling more comfortably isolated under their low-hanging cover. I noticed a thirties-something woman walking the cobblestones along the face of the Wall, apparently seeking ex-servicemen to engage. *She is a reporter*, I thought. She stared at me for a moment and I hung back. I did not need this. For me, this encounter was a spiritual union with my dead brothers, not an opportunity to help the American people put the Wall and the war in perspective.

Seconds passed, and she turned her stare away toward other targets. I stayed in the trees, trying to take full measure of what was before me. After a short period, I walked to the cobblestone footway, and west to the panel with Jeff Riek's and Bob Mossgrove's names. I believe for most combatants, upon at least their first visit, the enormity of the loss chronicled on the Wall is overwhelming. It was no less for me. I found the names *Robert B Mossgrove… Jeffry R Riek*

A young girl in thought, visiting the Wall

etched high on Panel 13W Line 54, along with their comrades in the day order of their deaths, February 25, 1970.

There was a feeling of partial fulfillment with me after that visit. I was no longer in the military, an exit strategy called peace with honor had been invoked, and Viêt Nam was united. Sadly, though, unification was under a repressive and vindictive government. The American effort, both incredibly heroic and badly bungled, had failed. But not due to the incompetence of the American soldier.

A reflecting self-portrait in the Wall on Panel 13W, taken in 2010. The names of Robert B Mossgrove and Jeffry R Riek can be seen on Line 54 near the top of the tree reflection.

I place responsibility at the feet of the American and Vietnamese political leadership. They could not bring themselves to work together on equal terms to do the hard work of large-scale cooperative counter-insurgency by helping the riceroots people genuinely improve their lot. Corruption in the Vietnamese government was too entrenched. The United States had its need to be in charge. These were the cultural imperatives that stood in the way. The peasantry would have set aside the Hồ Chí Minh narrative to have demonstrably better lives for their families, building on the success of the Census Grievance program. Rooted in the Mekong Delta, a fresh wave of nationalism might have taken hold and grown north. That would have been the true Vietnamization of the war, the one Lieutenant Colonel Châu dreamed of, the one that never was.

Perhaps the Vietnamese men I fought with who remained behind, defending their country and way of life, survived the fighting and the "reeducation" camps. Perhaps they would eventually have peaceful and productive lives. Yeah, and I put the likelihood of that musing with my childhood aspiration to be Superman.

Now fifty years later, with the war behind me and still struggling to find its proper context, the need for answers lives on with my generation. *Why was the war not won?* Put another way, *what could the US have done differently to make the odds for success better?* Considering the requirements of a successful counterinsurgency effort in Southeast Asia as outlined by Sir Robert Thompson in 1965, the answers to the common post-war questions have greater clarity.

Multiple factors emerge from the muddle of opinion, from learned to uninformed, and in between. Here is my Monday morning quarterbacking based on experience and influenced by Châu and Thompson. If the US had

- Supported the Vietnamese who proved the success of hearts-and-minds programs like the Static Census Grievance by insisting the GVN widely expand these programs as the solution to drive the Việt Cộng out of the villages and hamlets.

- Invested more in advisor training, both language and cultural sensitivity, and considered increasing the advisor tour length to eighteen or twenty-four months.
- Established counter Việt Cộng Infrastructure programs such as Phoenix much earlier in the Việt Cộng insurgency life-cycle.
- Established better intelligence coordination, synthesis, and rapid distribution methods.
- Emphasized to US commanders their need to operate in the background from the Vietnamese, particularly regarding pacification efforts.
- Understood that counterinsurgency was a war for the hearts and minds of the people, and that it would be a war of attrition where the winner was the one who outlasted his opponent.

Chapter 23

In the Closet with Carnivore

As the years went by, I found I was isolating more, completely avoiding social events, and mentally stiff-arming all thoughts of Việt Nam. I continued working in my own companies, taking contracts when the debts mounted up, finally establishing a one-man consulting business. I specialized in MS-DOS, Windows, device drivers, and very high-speed pattern matching technology development services. I enjoyed about a decade of being one of the experts who came in and helped the Washington, DC beltway bandits fulfill the contracts they had won. They put my quirks, most prominently blue jeans and a ponytail, down to typical guru behavior. When needed, I delivered in spades, and that was all they really cared about. But as the years went on, and my disorder progressed, completing tasks became more and more of a problem. I was developing indifference to consequences. I had to make a change or risk professional suicide.

In late 1998, I discarded my hired gun shingle and joined Sparta, a Tysons Corner, Virginia R & D firm that supplied contract development services to government organizations around the Washington, DC suburbs. Marketwise, it was a good fit for me as they had contracts with intelligence and law enforcement organizations and operated in the black project world I knew well. In their words, I had hit a home run in the hiring interview, excelling in one-on-one meetings, contrary to my disabling psych issues of a group setting. And they underscored why I knew I needed to get back to a job where I could lose myself in the gears of technology, innovating, where the PTSD anxiety had fewer chances to appear.

My first task with my new employer was a design and programming challenge for the Data Intercept Technology Unit (DITU) at a covert FBI structure known as the Stafford Pointe offsite extension of the Engineering Research Facility (ERF), located in Stafford, Virginia. I was pleased to get the job because working for the FBI had been an unrealized lifelong dream and it fit in with my counterintelligence background.

The FBI wanted a follow-on product to their Omnivore software for email network packet filtering and capture to help in the conviction of criminal elements operating in the United States, including those involved with terrorism, child pornography or exploitation, espionage, information warfare, and fraud. They expressed concerns about the limitations of the Omnivore software and wanted the new product as soon as possible. Not exactly a troubleshooting job, but close enough. I was in.

The design and implementation of the core of the new product was completely my call. The Bureau added a controlling front end and named the system Carnivore. As discussed with me, they wanted a reliable product running under Windows NT that was faster filtering network packets than the previous one. Omnivore, as I recall, was a port of code from a larger machine and was not known for its speed or precision.

This was my kind of challenge. I designed and developed the engine technology to intercept and filter the network packets, and an API to allow an application program to interface with it, calling upon its services. All that was needed to complete a Carnivore software product was the user front-end.

That interface component was developed in Visual Basic by Mason McDaniel, an uncommonly knowledgeable and professional young man whose skill set seemed to have no bounds. Mason was the FBI program manager for Carnivore and, as of this writing, is the chief technology officer at the Bureau of Alcohol, Tobacco, and Firearms (ATF), a federal law enforcement organization within the United States Department of Justice.

I placed the filtering engine and packet buffering in a network interface card device driver, a pioneering approach that promised to dramatically improve the filtering capacity of the technology. I initially named the package of these two components TapNdis, used in FBI operations, and then named the enhanced successor product FirstLight. The API was written as a Windows library known as a DLL, providing entry points for subroutine calls into the engine functionality. Both components I wrote in the "C" and "C++" language, although I paid close attention to the assembly code the compiler generated and made by-hand machine code replacements of the "C" code where necessary to improve performance.

I enjoyed a mutually respectful, professional, and friendly relationship with Mason and his boss, Jeff Eisensmith. I liked them both personally. Jeff believed in giving me latitude in my work for them, which I needed to perform, and his moments of occasional celebratory *happy dance* levity were always welcome. They were the kind of men I envisioned the Bureau would have as technical employees, the kind I liked to work with. To keep the relationship well-oiled, and to keep them informed about potential technology advances and impacts on our work, I would occasionally send a heads-up memo to them of what I saw around the technology corner.

One of the memos I sent discussed an emerging technology in the context of recent results of our internal throughput testing. When I had completed the first release of the TapNdis software, our in-house performance metrics clocked it as being more than eight times faster than the two best-selling *packet sniffers* on the market. But the testing results detailed in the aforementioned memo made my socks roll up and down.

It was a full-on bat-out-of-hell, approaching two orders of magnitude faster than its commercial competition, capable of capturing nearly anything on a gigabit link. In its proper court-ordered use, it would target only alleged criminals. In one unfortunate event in the Bureau's laboratory, however, this practice was ignored.

Sparta conducted performance tests on its TapNdis.sys protocol driver and TapApi.dll application program interface.

Scenario: The tests were run on a 450 MHz single processor PC under Windows NT/SP5. The test consisted of passing packets from a resident software packet generator directly to the TapNdis driver at the point of data entry from the NDIS layer, and timing the packets as they were filtered and presented to the user level application program. Both the packet generator and the user application (that read the packets from the driver/API, simulating real world use) ran concurrently with the TapNdis driver and TapApi API on the same single CPU system. TapNdis.sys was given a 16 MB internal buffer. Relevant packet yield was set at 100 percent of generated traffic.

Results: The results achieved—directly related to CPU bandwidth—were 800 Mbps sustained throughput (0.8 gigabits) with the traffic filters fully engaged searching for a specific TCP/IP port and address range combination.

I was running a test on a component of FirstLight, the future Carnivore engine. I had programmed into it the capability to search any binary (or text) stream within a network packet. The claim to fame of the technique I employed was that the time required to search for a pattern was extremely fast, and yet was not sensitive to the number of search target patterns because the pattern search was done *in parallel.* In other words, the time it took to search thousands of patterns was as fast as the time to search a single one.

"Bruce" was a brusk mover and shaker on the FBI intercept deployment team, those men and women who took Carnivore into the field to an ISP to collect digital traffic on a court-ordered surveillance subject. He was present in the lab when I was pre-alpha testing this part of the new FirstLight engine to be incorporated into Carnivore when it was fully debugged. He overheard me talking with a technician and asked if he could run a quick pattern matching test with the engine that was still under development. I was on respectful terms with the entire team, but I wanted to foster better relations with the deployment folks, so I saw no harm in following his informal request. I thought it particularly important because I was aware of ongoing disharmony between my FBI supervisors and Bruce, and this cooperation from me might help ease that.

Carnivore achieved its extraordinarily high throughput rate by a careful device driver design (TapNdis and FirstLight) around the system calls that pulled packets from the network interface card (NIC). By allocating a large buffer in kernel memory and passing back to the user a pointer to multiple packets on a single call, I realized many economies of scale. Most important of the savings was the dramatic reduction in CPU overhead time by eliminating a large number of user-to-kernel and kernel-to-user mode transitions.

He took the disk from me and disappeared for about fifteen minutes. When he returned, he had a big smile on his face and announced, "I just typed in seventy-five email addresses and it searched all of them without slowing down!" I nodded an acknowledgment; it did exactly what it was supposed to do. But then he floored me with his next statement. He said with emphasis: "I ran it against a live feed. That was with real traffic."

As I understood it, the Bureau considered it a serious breach of procedure to run a tap against live network traffic without a court order. Yet Bruce had done, by his own admission, exactly that. It disturbed me to realize both my company and I were unwittingly involved in what appeared to be a highly questionable action. Perhaps there was a legitimate explanation. But if so, it was not forthcoming.

I said nothing to Mason or Jeff of the irregularity. They were out of town, and I did not want to add fuel to the fire. About a week after the lab test, I received a call from Bruce at my company. He asked me for cooperation in applying the pre-alpha release—*an undebugged product*—for a use he did not specify. With this request coming on the heels of the still unexplained casual test the previous week, I gave the answer no one gives to the FBI who intends to continue to work for them. Much to the shock of my naturally accommodating boss, Mark, who did not realize the ramifications of Bruce's request, I gave an emphatic "no." There was no way, of course, I intended to involve myself or my company in Bruce's apparent off-the-reservation adventurism. His voice suddenly went cold, as if I had killed his dog or something. He had found my response unacceptable.

The shift in rapport had upset Mark, believing I had harmed the relationship. And, as it turned out, indeed I had. I called Bruce back a week later, inviting a compromise, but he was not having it. And I was okay with that. If the cost of business with the deployment group was acquiescing to ethical challenges, I was giving it a pass. I had a great reason: to protect myself, my company, and the customer from the risks of putting an undebugged product into use. Bruce knew better. It was unprofessional and simply not done.

Early in its life, Carnivore's existence and use at different ISP locations were considered sensitive, and consequently, not discussed with contractors or other outside personnel. Someone in the Bureau hierarchy, however, ordered a briefing on Carnivore for the visiting Congressman Bob Barr (R, GA). Then, by many accounts, the fur began to fly. There were a lot of chagrinned legislators on the Hill in DC, acting as if they had not heard of Carnivore, or so they said. The press, who were wild-eyed about this new FBI crime tool's ability to *scan millions of emails per second*, had a field day. Even more over-the-top was how upset privacy advocates became, erroneously asserting everyone's emails were being spied upon. But, for us at Sparta, secrecy was the watchword and my company division head directed that publicly discussing Carnivore by any of us would result in a personal fine payable to the company of $5,000.00.

The anger from the public over the privacy issues was misplaced but led eventually to congressional investigative hearings and a widely publicized formal technical review and testing of the Carnivore software. The Senate Judiciary committee convened a hearing in room SD-226 of the Dirksen Senate Office Building in early September 2000, one year before the 9/11 tragedy. Dr. Donald Kerr, FBI Assistant Director, was called to testify on "The 'Carnivore' Controversy: Electronic Surveillance and Privacy in the Digital Age."

Senator Orrin G. Hatch, Chairman, opened the meeting. "We are happy to welcome all of you out to today's hearing. The purpose of our hearing today is to examine the effect that new surveillance technologies, such as the FBI's now too famous Carnivore, is having on the important public policy balance between personal privacy rights and law enforcement in the digital age."

FBI's system to covertly search e-mail raises privacy, legal issues

By Neil King Jr. and Ted Bridis
THE WALL STREET JOURNAL

WASHINGTON, July 11 — The U.S. Federal Bureau of Investigation is using a superfast system called Carnivore to covertly search e-mails for messages from criminal suspects.

ESSENTIALLY A PERSONAL COMPUTER stuffed with specialized software, Carnivore represents a new twist in the federal government's fight to sustain its snooping powers in the Internet age. But in employing the system, which can scan millions of e-mails a second, the FBI has upset privacy advocates and some in the computer industry. Experts say the system opens a thicket of unresolved legal issues and privacy concerns.

The FBI developed the Internet wiretapping system at a special agency lab at Quantico, Va., and dubbed it Carnivore for its ability to get to "the meat" of what would otherwise be an enormous quantity of data. FBI technicians unveiled the system to a roomful of astonished industry specialists here two weeks ago in order to steer efforts to develop standardized ways of complying with federal wiretaps. Federal investigators say they have used Carnivore in fewer than 100 criminal cases since its launch early last year.

Word of the Carnivore system has disturbed many in the Internet industry because, when deployed, it must be hooked directly into Internet service providers' computer networks. That would give the government, at least theoretically, the ability to eavesdrop on all customers' digital communications, from e-mail to online banking and Web surfing.

The system also troubles some Internet service providers, who are loath to see outside software plugged into their systems. In many cases, the FBI keeps the secret Carnivore computer system in a locked cage on the provider's premises, with agents making daily visits to retrieve the data captured from the provider's network. But legal challenges to the use of Carnivore are few, and judges' rulings remain sealed because of the secretive nature of the investigations.

Internet wiretaps are conducted only under state or federal judicial order, and occur relatively infrequently. The huge majority of wiretaps continue to be the traditional telephone variety, though U.S. officials say the use of Internet eavesdropping is growing as everyone from drug dealers to potential terrorists begins to conduct business over the Web.

> Word of the Carnivore system has disturbed many in the Internet industry because, when deployed, it must be hooked directly into Internet service providers' computer networks.

The pre-9/11 atmosphere was strongly tilted toward the argued Fourth Amendment privacy rights of individuals. Dr. Kerr and his testifying associates were "beat up on" by some of the questioners as seen by my younger daughter Wendy, a psychology student at George Mason University, who unknown to me, attended the hearing as an observer. She had a protective interest in her dad as a combat veteran, having completed a term project on my wartime work as an

The FBI defends Carnivore as more precise than Internet wiretap methods used in the past. The bureau says the system allows investigators to tailor an intercept operation so they can pluck only the digital traffic of one person from among the stream of millions of other messages. An earlier version, aptly code-named Omnivore, could suck in as much as to six gigabytes of data every hour, but in a less discriminating fashion.

Still, critics contend that Carnivore is open to abuse.

Mark Rasch, a former federal computer-crimes prosecutor, said the nature of the surveillance by Carnivore raises important privacy questions, since it analyzes part of every snippet of data traffic that flows past, if only to determine whether to record it for police.

"It's the electronic equivalent of listening to everybody's phone calls to see if it's the phone call you should be monitoring," Mr. Rasch said. "You develop a tremendous amount of information."

Others say the technology dramatizes how far the nation's laws are lagging behind the technological revolution. "This is a clever way to use old telephone-era statutes to meet new challenges, but clearly there is too much latitude in the current law," said Stewart Baker, a lawyer specializing in telecommunications and Internet regulatory matters.

Robert Corn-Revere, of the Hogan & Hartson law firm here, represented an unidentified Internet service provider in one of the few legal fights against Carnivore. He said his client worried that the FBI would have access to all the e-mail traffic on its system, raising dire privacy and security concerns. A federal magistrate ruled against the company early this year, leaving it no option but to allow the FBI access to its system.

"This is an area in desperate need of clarification from Congress," said Mr. Corn-Revere.

"Once the software is applied to the ISP, there's no check on the system," said Rep. Bob Barr (R., Ga.), who sits on a House judiciary subcommittee for constitutional affairs. "If there's one word I would use to describe this, it would be 'frightening.'"

Marcus Thomas, chief of the FBI's Cyber Technology Section at Quantico, said Carnivore represents the bureau's effort to keep abreast of rapid changes in Internet communications while still meeting the rigid demands of federal wiretapping statutes. "This is just a very specialized sniffer," he said.

He also noted that criminal and civil penalties prohibit the bureau from placing unauthorized wiretaps, and any information gleaned in those types of criminal cases would be thrown out of court. Typical Internet wiretaps last around 45 days, after which the FBI removes the equipment. Mr. Thomas said the bureau usually has as many as 20 Carnivore systems on hand, "just in case."

FBI experts acknowledge that Carnivore's monitoring can be stymied with computer data such as e-mail that is scrambled using powerful encryption technology. Those messages still can be captured, but law officers trying to read the contents are "at the mercy of how well it was encrypted," Mr. Thomas said.

Most of the criminal cases where the FBI used Carnivore in the past 18 months focused on what the bureau calls "infrastructure protection," or the hunt for hackers, though it also was used in counterterrorism and some drug-trafficking cases.

"It's the electronic equivalent of listening to everybody's phone calls to see if it's the phone call you should be monitoring," Mr. Rasch said. "You develop a tremendous amount of information."

advisor. Wendy saved memorabilia I was going to throw out because they were too distracting for me to deal with at the time. Thanks, Wendy! They were, of course, invaluable in stimulating memories to include in this book.

At the time of the hearing, Wendy focused on Carnivore as an aid to federal law enforcement vis-a-vis privacy-related issues. After the session had completed, she followed Dr. Kerr into the hallway and walked with him as he made his way to the building entrance. In a brief conversation, she let him know that there was support for the FBI's position on Carnivore in the community. The Library of Congress houses the transcript to the Carnivore Senate hearing:

https://www.loc.gov/law/find/hearings/pdf/00089583263.pdf

The IIT Research Institute (IITRI) and the Illinois Institute of Technology Chicago-Kent College of Law were selected for the formal review task. As their "Independent Technical Review of the Carnivore System" report details, a comprehensive source code review and testing found no failures or bugs in the TapNdis device driver and its component API software. Further, it found no evidence of incorrect collection, either too much or too little of what was asked. Salient portions from the IITRI report:

> "IITRI determined that Carnivore, when properly configured under a Title III order, does not over-collect."

> "IITRI attempted to determine the throughput capacity of Carnivore both experimentally and analytically. Experimental attempts failed to drive sufficient traffic across the local area network to make Carnivore drop packets; traffic never reached the point where packets were dropped."

This finding was consistent with our extensive testing at Sparta, performed nightly against our own company network. Carnivore's bonafides as a solid piece of crime-fighting software were undisputed. Nonetheless, I had more than a few sleepless nights of concern over being called before Congress to testify in the mother of all briefings, as the Carnivore engine developer. But both my company and the FBI protected the identity of their personnel, so my anxiety illness was not significantly aggravated. Indeed, judging by the IITRI report, there is no indication anyone outside the FBI was involved in developing the Carnivore engine.

As the development of the Carnivore 2 engine, FirstLight, was well underway and I was testing components of the product at the DITU lab, a supervisory special agent approached me and introduced himself. "Kent" was extremely interested in Carnivore, its future capabilities, and its scheduled completion date. He was an enigmatic man, not given to saying more than necessary, or showing much emotion. In the time I knew him, I saw him crack a smile only once. That was the day he approached me in the lab and asked me about the product schedule. Kent seemed accepting of my answers, then he asked me what name I wanted for the new release of Carnivore. It surprised me for two reasons. First, the Bureau had renamed Carnivore the innocuous-sounding *DCS-1000.* Second, he was appearing to offer me the opportunity to name it.

I told Kent that I did not have a suggested name to replace the DCS-1000 moniker, but that my wife had an idea. He leaned forward slightly, and I knew I had him. This was going to be a hoot. With perfect diction and enunciation, I offered "Consider changing the name D-C-S-One-Zero-Zero-Zero to R-I-N-One-Zero-One-Zero." He squinted seeking understanding. I paused for effect. "Rin-Tin-Tin," I deadpanned. Kent, in true agent style, tried hard to avoid revealing emotion, but he was caught off-guard. He brought his hand to his mouth, trying to muffle the laughter, but only with partial success. That was my sole relaxed moment with Kent.

Around DITU, it was no secret how much I admired the Bureau and the folks who worked for them. Late one morning, about a week following the DCS-1000 renaming goofiness, Kent was giving me a lift to their division headquarters at Quantico. I was scheduled to meet for lunch with my Sparta boss, who was there for a meeting.

As we were traveling, Kent glanced over from the driver's seat and asked me if my wife and I would like to go to dinner with him and his wife. *Oh, wow.* This was a terrifically bad idea. I believe

Kent was going to feel me out on possibly coming to work for the Bureau. Up to this point, Carnivore was flying sky-high, and my political capital seemed unlimited. But my great weakness was about to be uncovered. My ability to sit down and enjoy a simple meal with people had been eroding since returning from Viêt Nam. It was another aspect of the combat PTSD where I could not feel safe, provoking extreme anxiety, agitation, and a fight-or-flight response. But all I could do about it was to avoid the situation.

In the past, I had paid dearly in relationships for not attending social events, particularly those involving meals. Once a former employer wanted to take a few coworkers and me to a farewell lunch, but I demurred. He was aghast that I would refuse, and of course, I would tell no one the true reason for my behavior.

In this case with Kent, it was I who was caught off-guard. I was surprised into silence at his request. There was an uncomfortable dead air between us until we arrived at Quantico. *How could I explain this?* There was not an out for me. I would not share the fact of my illness with my contemporaries. As I had in the past, I accepted the appearance of rudeness as part of who I had to be to get by.

In the spring of 2001, I was living at my home in Venice, Florida and commuting to the FBI in Virginia once every six weeks. I enjoyed the productive atmosphere of my at-home computer lab, having no requirement to interface with anyone. I was abundantly aware of our country's focus on Osama bin Laden and the FBI's stated possible use of Carnivore in counterterrorism efforts.

Personally, as a former counter-intelligence type, I tended to notice things that were *unusual* or *out of place*. In my business of software development, though, I was nowhere near the investigations side of things within the Bureau, except to provide a useful tool for digital evidence collection. But like many people, I did notice uncommon circumstances in everyday life and tended to retain that information.

As US attorney's general have reinforced, the government, in the pursuit of justice, does not engage in racial profiling. That is, for example, they would not have a valid predicate to open a counter-intelligence investigation into someone based solely on a person's ethnicity. But they do have the authority to collect information to determine if an investigation should be opened. A good example of information collection, purely serendipitous, illustrates the point. Late one morning, probably in April 2001, we had completed brunch at The Clock restaurant. Working from home in Venice had allowances such as sporadic meals at "safe" places, at which I managed an acceptable comfort level. My wife enjoyed the meals out, infrequent as they were. This restaurant in Venice was such a breakfast place for us. I paid our bill, and we walked out and into the parking lot. While standing beside our car, I noticed a convertible driving north on business Route 41 that had stopped for a nearby traffic light. It was a highly unusual scene for Venice because the car had its top down and carried five or six passengers. Most were bearded and wearing

My computer lab at home in Venice, Florida, 2001

head coverings fashioned as turbans. Their collective appearance was one of seemingly wanting to be on display, which I also regarded as uncommon. Arab men were typically much more circumspect. While this was about five months before 9/11, but with bin Laden's general intentions known to the Intelligence Community, it struck me that these gentlemen almost seemed to be parading their ethnicity, as if trying to hide in plain sight.

While some might say it was a stretch that they appeared out of place, I had not seen more than one or two Arab men, much less riding together in an open convertible, in the many years I had visited and lived in Venice. My counterintelligence background had kicked in and I considered passing the information along to my contacts at the FBI. At the end of the day, though, I decided it was too flimsy an observation, without sufficient foundation, to bother them with.

Reflecting on it now in the full context of the 9/11 plot, these men conceivably could have been some of the hijackers who we now know did frequent a bar next to the Venice Airport. At the moment I saw the men, they were heading in a direction away from the local airport and the Venice library, where the hijackers trained and used publicly available computers for Internet access. Conversely, they could have been ordinary citizens or visitors minding their own business, rightly expecting the government to do the same.

Despite the successes of Carnivore, by mid-June 2001 my productivity had noticeably slowed. Worse, my programming effort on the follow-on release of Carnivore became spurty, pushing through hastily during periods of forced higher output. This led to a logic oversight and the introduction of a readily visible bug in a test version of the software. It was unrelated to the packet filtering but eroded my influence at the Bureau nonetheless. The work on the unreleased product was at least two months past its due date, the deployment lead was down on all things Carnivore, and the public and Congress were still upset over its alleged legendary capabilities.

The development delays were due mostly to me underscoping the requirements' workload and, of course, the personal anxiety challenges. The Bureau necessarily continued to expend a lot of resources managing the Carnivore publicity fallout and was becoming weary of this need. Some in the Bureau were even beginning to question whether future releases of Carnivore would be more of a metaphorical boat anchor than a nimble digital evidence collection tool.

In the release of the new Carnivore engine that I named First-Light, I had been tasked to significantly expand the filtering intercept capabilities. To meet that need without compromising performance, I planned to use the Intel CPU's specialized MMX hardware. That final step was never realized, however, as the deployment folks won the day, and the development project was brought to a halt.

> The new FirstLight device driver would include more parallelism by vectorizing the filtering request and employing deterministic finite automata. The process was implemented with a temporary software routine that would later be replaced, after full debugging, with the Intel Pentium CPU architecture MMX instruction set, supporting high-speed 64-bit vector operations. MMX was a single instruction, multiple data (SIMD) instruction set with directly addressable registers, introduced a few years earlier.

Mark and I were called in to a meeting that morning with Jeff and Mason, both looking somber and disappointed. Jeff did the talking and gave the official position of the Bureau on why the project was shutting down. He was polite but firm, always the professional, informing us it was over. They both left the meeting after delivering the news without having sat down or soliciting a response from us. It came as no surprise to me, aware of the considerable intersectional rivalry, and sway of the strong forces in deployment and their expanding reach into the FBI hierarchy. Ever since I rebuffed Bruce's cowboy behavior months earlier, the deployment folks wanted to replace Carnivore with commercial software. I took the official reason relayed by Jeff more as a demonstration of that influence from the higher-ups than a genuine one.

Mark appeared shocked, uncertain what to do or say. I turned toward him in my seat and offered what I hoped was useful guidance. "Have you ever been involved with a project that was shut down?" He shook his head *no*. "What people remember is how you conducted yourself," I advised. We accepted what they said, stood up, and left the building. That was the end of my work for the Bureau, for then. I returned a few years later to work on an even more covert project.

To my knowledge, FirstLight was easily the most sophisticated and capable packet sniffing product coming to market in 2001. Had the development effort been better scoped, had the deployment team been more on-board, and had the putative shortcomings of the current release of Carnivore been addressed and resolved, the advanced FirstLight engine would have seen service.

Chapter 24
The Last Hurrah

One of the men I worked with at the Quantico, Virginia FBI facility left the Bureau and went to work for a Los Angeles company in their defense division. I was employed with a four-man firm in Stafford, under contract to a different group within the FBI. These were the folks who reportedly developed the Magic Lantern software for the Bureau. The work and my teammates were enjoyable and even more hush-hush than Carnivore. However, there was no future for me here, given my age of fifty-six and the small company's lack of a retirement participation plan. The former Bureau employee got in touch with me and suggested I meet with the Los Angeles organization to decide if we were a fit.

At first, I was reluctant to consider working for a large company. My working life after Viêt Nam was with small organizations, most that I created, so I could carefully place myself in a position to minimize the intense anxiety from interacting with people. I thought perhaps this job with a smaller group within the large company just might work out. My interview in Anaheim, California with the defense firm went extremely well. It was another home run. I liked the two bosses I met. We negotiated an offer; the deal was sealed, and Terrie and I moved west.

I had every reason to think my job at the defense company would be applying the high-speed packet intercept know-how I developed.

But they apparently were confused about my job interests. Instead, while giving me a free hand, they tried to put me in competition with another employee for supervising the new Information Operations lab they were establishing. During the interview process, I had made it clear to them I had no intention of performing as a manager. This was something I knew I could not do, being subject to bouts of severe anxiety and hypervigilance when required to speak to groups of any size. It disappointed me that they now wanted me to have a much more visible and supervisory position than I had negotiated—an uncomfortable beginning.

Early in my work for the West Coast company, an opportunity presented itself to debug three intractable software integration problems at their affiliate in Australia. I had been to Sydney in 1970, on R & R from Viêt Nam, and loved the place. I could not pass up this software troubleshooting opportunity and the chance to live in Brisbane for three months while I sought solutions for these few but longstanding critical problems. This would be a temporary assignment, and I believed I could shield myself from interactions with most people. And on the technical side, the Aussies were a competent group of developers and integrators but did not have the depth of familiarity with Windows I did. I asked to go, was selected, and left with Terrie for three months TDY.

As good luck would have it, I solved Persistent Problem One on the first day of my assignment. They were using third party software to manage multiple connections of a communications program and found the calls unexpectedly being closed seemingly at random without action on their part. It smelled like a *critical section* problem in this multi-threaded environment, so I suggested the operator restart Windows in single-threaded mode to see if the problem continued. He was unfamiliar with that option and the command line argument for it under Windows but was eager to give it a go. He cranked it up, and the problem went away, confirming my belief that the vendor had a logic hole in their program's semaphore handling. I wrote a brief email to the vendor, who was able to quickly reproduce the problem and isolate the error. An updated application program from the vendor was available the next day.

Persistent Problem Two was solved about a week later, bringing my status among the Aussies to that of a demigod. Solving the three problems were critical to the successful completion of their contract, and we were well on our way. Persistent Problem Three was solved weeks later by one of the Australians, and I was pleased to see it. The nature of it was out of my area of concentration, so I particularly appreciated his help and success.

We loved the time we spent in Australia, a once-in-a-lifetime opportunity. They put us up in a charming apartment right on the Brisbane River. But the three months in Brissey went by quickly, and all too soon it was time to pack up and head home to Anaheim.

The Brisbane River from our apartment

I did much of my kind of work at the defense company in a SCIF, a Sensitive Compartmented Information Facility. Basically, we worked in a vault. Occasionally, char personnel, who normally were not cleared for this level of classified information to be in the SCIF, were brought in for brief periods to vacuum floors and collect the trash. As is commonplace in such situations, management sounded an alerting audible alarm whenever the char folks entered the SCIF. For me, though, it was most unfortunate. The SCIF warning was a 1950s air-raid siren-sounding alert that closely resembled the Tân Trụ compound siren, indicating a possible enemy attack was underway.

I was already in trouble psychologically, finding myself trying to meet job requirements in larger and larger crowds, as the project grew. I became easily agitated, continually working in fight-or-flight situations. I slept poorly and was not trusting anyone. I was scrutinizing every person I faced with friend-or-harmful-foe uncertainty, and considerable unease. I became badly hypervigilant and was visibly startled nearly every time I exited the SCIF when meeting someone immediately on the opposing side of the door waiting to walk in. My jumpiness became a topic of conversation among my peers, and that observation further isolated me. And now, the siren pulled me back halfway around the world, directly to the compound, and its risks of living and fighting in Viêt Nam.

I found myself plagued with what I called brain fog, an inability to concentrate, or dependably recall either short- or long-term memories. It alarmed me that I could not remember some more advanced computer science fundamentals. I had to fix this problem as quickly as I could, so I applied for acceptance in the Viterbi School of Engineering at the University of Southern California (USC). They admitted me into the grad school's master's program in computer science. I was able to take, on an after-hours basis, three courses. I averaged an A- in the classes and that helped my confidence and retention of computer science know-how.

The second most difficult problem I faced was a type of aphasia, a condition where communication — in my case, speech — was affected. If it was a briefing or a meeting, I was in trouble. To deal with this psych issue head on, but still not fully connecting it with the true source of the problem, I joined the company's Toastmasters group and met three times with them. They were keenly interested in helping me, but after a few encounters, I saw that my issues were much more deep-seated than this well-intentioned organization could solve.

An unexpected predicament was my loss of driving skill. While in control of the car, too many things seemed to be happening at once. I could not mentally process it quickly enough to drive, or even to do something otherwise relatively simple such as changing lanes on a moderately crowded interstate. The risk to safety became too great. It was not long before my wife did all the driving to work and to my weekly Anaheim combat PTSD veteran's meetings. This depressed me even more, adding to the already increased burden Terrie had taken on.

I had, some months earlier, driven to the Long Beach VA Hospital for help in understanding what I was going through. The only evidence that I had of a possible Việt Nam combat connection was the nightmares and some intrusive daytime thoughts. I did not yet believe I had PTSD. The VA hospital had a walk-in clinic that welcomed Việt Nam vets with psych issues. They funneled me in and ninety minutes later, spit me out with psych medications and a diagnosis of severe combat PTSD.

The intake physician's assistant told me my adrenalin levels were extraordinarily high, my pupils were dilated, and anxiety and hyper vigilance were apparent. Her pink coiffure could not belie her professional competence as she pointedly encouraged me to apply for disability compensation from Veterans Affairs. "It is not just for the guys who have lost an arm or leg. You should apply. I know you PTSD guys don't feel you are injured. But you are. Make the call. You have earned it." As I thought seriously about applying for more help, she gave me the contact point for an Anaheim-based combat veterans' PTSD group that met weekly. They, in turn, referred me to the VA Mood Disorders Clinic in Anaheim. I was beginning to feel hopeful.

But hope was short-lived. Over the next few months, my ability to cope with the requirements of the job deteriorated. The fight-or-flight response was becoming more intense. There were times when I was approached by a few people among the cubicles who wanted to caucus on a technical issue but would crowd too close to me. The tension became so great, I was concerned I might physically push them back away from me. Of course, physical contact against another employee was not only patently wrong, it was also a firing offense. I had to protect them and myself from this aspect of the fight-or-flight behavior.

I came up with an ad hoc solution that worked well. The issue of me getting physical was made moot, and it gave me a sense of calm that allowed a closer focus on the technical discussion. After all, that was the reason I was there. The answer was simple. I put each hand in its respective back pocket of my close-fitting blue jeans and made fists. This action made my hands too large to remove impulsively from my jean back pockets. Over the last few months of my employ, I quietly applied this technique many times.

In some ways, the company gave me a lot of latitude and relief from responsibilities in dealing with the PTSD manifestations. Thanks go to supervisors Haig and Ron, in particular. But lethargy was becoming a larger part of the syndrome, and as many as a third of the employees were much less thoughtful. I saw everything from looks of disdain to eye-rolling to outright laughter. I became aware that well poisoning had occurred from a small clique of secretaries, the backbone of the department, who could not appreciate my difficulty. The situation was depressing, and it was not improving. It had been made personal now, and on-the-job tolerance from some coworkers I was asked to caucus with was not to be found.

The tasking shifted, and Ron directed me, along with two other people, to each provide a draft of a white paper on a topic related to the work under contract in this SCIF. My write-up was original and well received, but it opened a can of worms for me. The research uncovered a potential weakness in the primary product under development in this SCIF. I wrote a follow-on white paper, "Detecting … Through TCP Discontinuities," expressing in detail my concern with the SCIF product technical weakness I alleged. Sadly, I could not interest my managers in reading it. The department, eager to win the project's technical competition with other companies, indicated to me they would address the issue in the next phase of the product's development. But by this time and owing to their poor responsiveness to the issue I'd raised, I had less confidence in the company management and their ability to meet their expressed intention. It was a particularly egregious situation because if they confirmed the weakness, the safety of American combat soldiers was at risk. One of my managers openly laughed at that prospect when I brought it up to him. For me, the responsibility to preserve combatant safety easily eclipsed all others.

My apprehension became so great that I eventually reported failing to investigate my stated concerns as an ethics violation to the appropriate group within the company. Prior to that action, I had invited scrutiny of my assertions from offsite, non-invested company employees with base knowledge of the underlying technology and issues I had discussed in my paper. I contended that my concerns, which I strongly believed to be valid, were not being given enough consideration. The company management would not agree, however, to a meeting between the offsite experts and me to discuss the issue. That fact became my tipping point.

Another of my managers, Fred, not involved in either product development or the ethics filing, took me to lunch and surprised me by asking the name of my VA psychiatrist. This manager had been an invaluable friend and supporter of my professional growth. I realized, though, Fred was a go-between. I judged one of his bosses had asked for the information. Nonetheless, I saw no reason not to share it. I was open to help and this might give the company more understanding and comfort about my mental health condition. I gave Fred the physician's name and his phone number.

But soon both the situation within the company and my personal well-being rapidly deteriorated, and I knew I had to medically retire. I could no longer fight this battle. I informed the company of my decision and gave them a termination date. On the chosen day, I out-processed and then reported for my wrap-up meeting with my VA psychiatrist, the chief of the Mood Disorders Clinic at the Long Beach VA hospital.

The doctor acted like a different man from the one I had met and talked at length with at our first meeting a few weeks earlier. It was but a few minutes into the discussion when I realized he no longer supported my claim with the VA for the PTSD diagnosis. This surprise stunned me. I had just retired from my job, my only source of income and paid medical care, and my VA physician was now dismissing my claim, one that they themselves had already diagnosed as severe PTSD.

I felt quite discouraged about this and discussed it with my VA group counselor. This therapist had talked with me many times over the previous months and had a better handle on evaluating my condition. Within a few days I received a call from my VA psychiatrist's office asking me to come in again. When I met with him this time, it was immediately clear he was angry. His upset was not with me, but with whoever had called his office a week earlier to allege I was not sick with PTSD at all.

Now it made sense. I remembered the friendly manager who had asked me to have lunch with him and then inquired of my VA doctor's name. This was sad, indeed, and a serious breach of the company's policy. It was a cardinal rule within that corporation that under no circumstances could there be retaliatory action taken toward an employee who filed an ethics grievance against one of his managers.

The meeting with my VA doctor ended after an hour. I thanked him for his diagnosis and help in supporting my claim for disability. He could not have agreed more, rating my Global Assessment of Functioning (GAF) at an exceedingly low number. Shortly thereafter, I began the move back to a safer place, my home in Florida. But the psych low point and loss of everyday skills continued. I could not tolerate the rapid movement of others around me, common household noises, or people talking within earshot for more than a few minutes at a time. Intimacy became essential for me to decompress.

When I arrived in Florida, I joined a combat PTSD group in nearby Sarasota and learned more about this disease and how others coped with it. A year later, the VA claims backlog had ebbed and reached my application. They awarded me a 100% schedular Permanent and Total rating for PTSD, the gold standard. They suggested, and we agreed, that a guardian should be appointed for custodial management of my finances. This process continued for two years, until through the pharmacological and counseling skill of my psychiatrist, Dr. Kayan, I showed enough signs of improvement to reassume my responsibilities.

My relationship with Terrie was reestablished, at a much deeper level. We both found intimacy the key for this PTSD veteran, as a new bedrock from which to rebuild a life. For me, it was digging even deeper into her psyche, relearning the things beyond her wants to her needs. This can be deeply personal, and not something readily divined or discussed between partners.

I found the intimacy renaissance so effective for both of us that I recommended to the vet center they consider adding a class on couple's intimacy to their standard relationship counseling and PTSD coping strategies courses. The approach I took was to do an interpersonal drill-down, appreciating the raw female-male visceral needs and then work to supply them.

As I was revisiting relationships and working through my PTSD issues, I unpacked some of my Viêt Nam memorabilia. My older daughter, Sarah, had a few years earlier in a "looking out for her dad" mission, independently set up scrap books and organized the materials. Thank you, Sarah! I had not been able to look closely at the souvenirs and awards since returning from overseas. It was a cathartic experience, feeling some pent-up release after being pulled back to that war zone by touching and reviewing the materials. But it was a good experience because I was now in a position, through my PTSD group sessions, to put the memorabilia in their proper context. I was still attached to them, but I was no longer pulled back *into* them. I had another life now, and it was not Viêt Nam.

The company I retired from before moving to Florida eventually stepped up, offering me both short-term and long-term disability, and a retirement stipend. That was fifteen years ago, and the combat veteran support group in Sarasota has helped enormously. Over the years in talking with other VA counselors, I have learned the Sarasota therapists are unique among VA PTSD groups. Their success record, established by and for many years under the leadership of Fred McLaughlin, is exemplary. I can enjoy some outside activities now, and my startle response is near normal. But I do prefer to stay indoors, and I feel safest when in group counseling with the other combatants, a condition not uncommon among Viêt Nam PTSD veterans.

Along the way, my PTSD group pulled me in for outside activities. Sail boating and whitewater rafting were two sports I could bring myself to try. PTSD-ers are emotionally numb from persistently high levels of adrenaline and will often seek risky activities to get adrenaline to "push through" at even higher levels so they can *feel* again.

The advanced whitewater run of the Upper Gauley in West Virginia was the rafting site with its famous 2,600 cfs flows. We made two trips down the thirteen-mile iconic class V rapids, one of the three highest-rated places in the United States for those into that kind of personal abuse. Gauley season is six weeks in September and October where the dam at Summersville Lake is released, supplying the best whitewater experience on the East Coast.

The photo sequence, taken by the rafting company photographer, shows my spill out of the raft at Class V Pillow Rock, and my pop-up appearance above water fifty meters downriver. The "fun" was to approach and ram the Pillow at relatively high speed, effecting a raft bounce-back from the rock. It had the unfortunate consequence of ejecting me and one other thrill-seeker into the narrow Pillow Rock channel of fast and deep whitewater, keeping us trapped under the surface. I did breathe in water that day, but people on a downstream raft noticed my distress, and a mesomorphic guy pulled me from the water. I lay flat on their boat and coughed for more than a few minutes. As if we needed confirmation of the fact, we learned firsthand the Upper Gauley is a dangerous whitewater experience. On average, it kills one person per season.

The first of two rapid runs. I am on the far left.

Boat Captain Thor Erickson owns the *Windependent*, a cutter-rigged sailboat, meaning it has a smaller sail in front of the mast and behind the foresail. On occasional times when the Gulf of Mexico weather was cooperating, he would collect a handful of us for a weekend getaway. We would cruise to and anchor in a SW Florida cove. This was great fellowship and allowed us to push the anxiety envelope safely in the company of other Viêt Nam combat veterans.

Thor and his wife, Lorraine, lobbied strongly for Terrie and me to go on an ocean cruise with them. We relented in 2009 and quickly became hooked. I found it was an ideal getaway for someone with PTSD anxiety issues. The times I felt like mixing it up, I could venture out of my cabin to little-used snack bars or restaurants. If I

Thor Erikson and Chris Keilty adjusting
the Windependent rigging

needed relief from the passengers, I could stay in my cabin and enjoy the scenery from our balcony with breakfast in bed. In ports of call, I could opt out of the trip ashore, or pick an excursion likely to be less crowded. Terrie played Mahjong, frequented the smorgasbords, and did international shopping to her heart's delight. Princess Cruises became our cruise line of choice, working well for us. We continued cruising until the end of 2015 when I found the manifestations of an encroaching metabolic disease made travel too difficult.

Paul Hansen defending against my ramming speed attack

Another getaway common among our veteran group was kayaking and fishing in the local Florida everglades. While I substituted my camera for a fishing rod on such ventures, the fellowship was tops as this photo of my friend and fellow Mekong combatant Paul Hansen suggests.

Paul was in-country from October 1967 to October 1968 in Long An province when it was fully under enemy control. He was an eleven-bravo squad leader with Bravo company of the US 3/39 in the 9th Infantry. His duty stations were Rạch Kiến and later Đồng Tâm, the first being on the northern border of Tân Trụ. Paul was wounded twice on January 8 and hospitalized for three weeks. He was sent back to his unit in time for the infamous Tet of 1968.

Relief from combat PTSD symptoms is itself an uncanny phenomenon. While difficult to explain precisely why, some of my PTSD group vets, Chris Keilty and Jim McSorley, have found a way out for brief periods with SCUBA diving. I had similar experiences when I was freediving—breath-hold diving beneath the waves with no sound, being able to peacefully integrate with schools of fish. Something about the sea; hard to explain, but it works. And I must parenthetically offer that when it comes to diving, SCUBA is blatant cheating. Imagine. Taking air underwater with you.

Wikipedia defines freediving as "any of various aquatic activities that share the practice of breath-hold underwater diving." For me, that activity was photography. With an underwater point-and-shoot Panasonic Lumix TS-2, I breath-held, dove to a coral reef, and snapped photos of fish and other aquatic creatures. I was a minimalist underwater photographer: no camera housing, no lights, and no air, with a camera watertight to about forty feet.

Quality underwater pix are difficult to get. Most are taken by SCUBA divers who use a large professional DSLR camera with a protective housing and external lights. These air breathers can patiently wait for a subject to move into the best position.

Conversely, freedivers have only a minute or so to get to depth, find the critter, line up the shot, and take it with whatever light is available. Longer breath-holds are key because many fish will allow you to integrate with them if you stay down long enough and avoid sudden moves.

Because of the lack of an air supply, freediving photographers rarely dive deeply, say below forty feet. Besides the obvious reason of the deeper the dive, the greater the overall need for air, colors disappear rapidly as one descends due to light refraction. At about forty feet, red, orange, and yellow have disappeared. Artificial lights are necessary to illuminate the subject and produce the color.

Training to freedive is essential before giving it a go. Practicing breath-holds under various conditions and depths is impor-tant—and always with a buddy. Wearing a lightweight wet suit, a small-capacity mask, long fins, and enough weight on a belt will push the odds toward safe, successful diving.

Freedivers keep track of their stats, their "personal best," if you will, of accomplishment. Each diver is different and trains to move the numbers in the direction that is most helpful for his need. Having mentioned that, here are my stats, satisfactory for a journeyman freediving photographer. Time is expressed as mm:ss.

Maximum breath-hold, out of water: 4:45.
Maximum breath-hold, underwater: 3:10.
Maximum underwater depth: 9 meters.
Distance covered in one minute of breath-hold, vigorous underwater finning: 50 meters.

If you wish to explore freediving, read up on it first. Here is the bible: *Manual of Freediving: Underwater on a Single Breath* by Umberto Pelizzari and Stefano Tovaglieri, available at amazon.com.

A final cautionary word, portions from Wikipedia: The experience of freedom in an underwater environment can make freediving an exhilarating personal and spiritual journey. Thus, it is especially attractive to young men, the segment of this sport with the greatest number of fatalities. If you wish to consider learning to freedive, remember that without proper training and supervision, freediving is exceedingly dangerous. With training, it is considered an extreme sport.

Chapter 25

The Endgame

Walking along the seventh-floor corridor to the elevator, I felt stunned beyond words. It was mid-morning on a Wednesday, and I had been seen by Dr. Hyde of a premier neurology practice in Sarasota, Florida. "If you have what I think you have, the outlook is grim," he declared. He was expressing his belief after completing an EMG/NCV examination, detailing how well the nerves and muscles in my legs and arms were functioning. The test provides inferential data on a possible diagnosis, revealing the impact characteristics of the disease for a professional interpretation.

Hyde was not forthcoming beyond his startling pronouncement, and I sat too shocked to pose follow-up questions. But Hyde prided himself on his expertise interpreting the neurophysiologic waveforms and discrete data, as he opined. He knew what he was talking about, and I was in trouble.

A half-hour later, I joined the men of my combat PTSD class for lunch, having missed the group session because of my medical appointment. Thor, a prominent member of the group and good friend, asked me how it went. "Nothing unusual. It all looked fine," I lied. I was still considering what I had been told. I was not yet ready to share it. Thor was a discerning man and did not readily accept what I told him. He must have picked up on a facial clue I was unaware I was giving.

"How did it go, Bob?" he asked again. I paused and gave the same reply. When he asked the third time, I shared the information with him. I quoted Hyde and took a seat at the lunch table. Nothing further was said about it as I went through the meal as if by rote.

I had another of my monthly meetings with Dr. Kayan a few days hence, and he immediately recognized the change in my demeanor. I shared Hyde's prediction with him. We talked it around, and he stressed the need to let the disease, whatever it might be, unfold itself, to not hurry it along. After all, Hyde's comment might be wide of the mark. Hope, he implied, was an important part of dealing with chronic disease.

It was weeks later that I learned a communication apparently had taken place between the two physicians. While this information was not offered, and I did not ask about it, Kayan apparently admonished Hyde for taking away hope in his unsolicited comment to me on the lethality of the disease. If it happened that way, it would have been classic Dr. Kayan. He was a legend among combat veterans for his ability to lessen the effects of PTSD, and to help us achieve more normal lives. I was aware he saw me as a potential suicide case. That must have been the reason for his call to Hyde. To the extent possible, he encouraged his combat PTSD veterans to keep the war in its proper context.

A month passed by, with me becoming more accepting of my forecast fate, and a follow-up meeting was due with Dr. Hyde. As I sat waiting for him in the small examination room, Hyde walked in. He shot me a focused icy stare, which told me he and Kayan indeed had words, and he was not happy about it. Deciding it was time to take his "grim" diagnosis to the next step, I asked about it. This time, however, he denied ever having made such a remark. *OK, I got it.* He was offering hot and steamy nonsense to cover himself. It was time, I now saw, to get another neurologist. I could no longer depend on Hyde.

While much of my time was spent researching the syndrome of my disease and learning how to talk with clinicians in their language to interest them in my case, I found my childhood fascination with photography had resurfaced. I bought a groundbreaking Sony NEX-5 camera, lightweight enough for me to handle without too much hand tremor and began shooting everything in sight. In 2010, I travelled to Washington, DC to visit my daughters and took many photos of the monuments. At home, I printed the keepers on 13" by 19" Hahnemühle Photo Rag photographic paper and put up a website on our offerings. Along with the support of a few other veterans—Thor

Erickson, Jimmy Lannon, and Paul Hansen, Purple Heart Viêt Nam vets all—I made trips to three of Florida's 120-bed VA nursing facilities. We gave to the patients over five hundred copies of the photos mounted on foam board for easy wall—or ceiling—hanging.

The photos given to the hospitalized veterans were a big hit. Like myself, the PTSD men among the patients found that the bright colors of the photographs helped distract from intrusive and disturbing thoughts, common among former combatants.

In 2011, I trekked to the Dry Tortugas in the westernmost islands of the Florida Keys. Reachable only by air or sea, I took a six-passenger puddle-jumping sea plane to Fort Jefferson. It is on a sixteen-acre island supporting the massive but unfinished nineteenth century coastal fortress. Fort Jefferson, a major tourist attraction, has played an even larger role in United States history. In July 1865, Dr. Samuel Mudd, convicted of conspiring to assassinate President Abraham Lincoln, was imprisoned there. Dr. Mudd, however, was subsequently pardoned by President Andrew Johnson.

One photograph I took at the fort was of a brick hallway, feeding a cannon emplacement area known as casemates. The fort wall

"Arches," the 2011 national award winner in the category of Color Photography

openings, called embrasures, made possible the large cannon firing positions to the sea. I felt the photo turned out particularly well, so I entered it in the Veterans Affairs 2011 national color photography contest. I saw it as a striking photo, and the judges apparently agreed, awarding it First Place in the competition of about 8,000 photographs. The appearance of three dimensions in the photo underscores the precision with which they constructed this fort of sixteen million bricks over a sandy island. After the award was announced, the *Journal of Rehabilitation Research and Development (JRRD)* contacted me to ask if I would agree to having the photo appear on their cover, along with a brief bio of me as a combat PTSD veteran. The winning photo and the *JRRD* cover and write-up are pictured here.

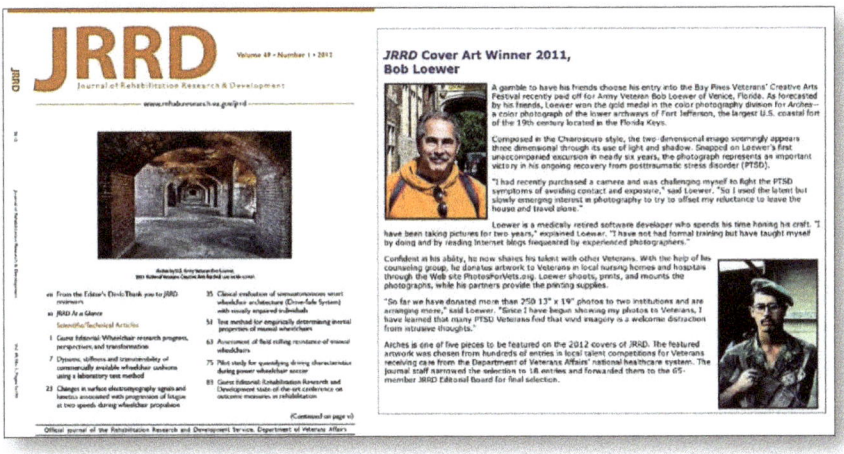

The Journal of Rehabilitation Research and Development, *published for decades, fell to the budget cutters' axe in 2017.*

The date February 14, 2014, has a permanent place in my memory. Not for a Valentine's Day celebration. But for the day I was given a five-year reprieve from the undiagnosed and debilitating physical illness I was now fully exhibiting. My neurological condition had rapidly deteriorated. I could not walk easily, often stumbling, and proper balance was difficult to maintain. I had a positive Romberg, which meant if I shut my eyes, I would fall over. The intentional hand tremor had become severe. It affected even gross motor movements as in raising a fork or glass to my mouth.

My clinicians, from every discipline imaginable, had seen nothing like the presentation of my disease. Over time, I learned that consuming carbohydrates worsened the disease. In practical terms, I could not eat carbohydrates without having a follow-up reaction of advancing distal numbness in my legs and arms, within hours of eating. Bloodwork was abnormal in several categories, confirming the presence of disease with unusual signs. Diabetes tests were negative. The clinical phenotype screamed the existence of a pathology, but no one had a clue.

I resisted the often-heard declaration among Việt Nam veterans that my disease must be agent orange related. While it is true that I encountered the organophosphate defoliant in Việt Nam, I did not want to make that assertion. Why? Because I knew that if clinicians, most of whom were poorly motivated to solve this clinical brainteaser, came to believe that agent orange poisoning was the probable cause, they would stop looking for a diagnosis and treatment. The neurological fingerprints of this dying-back axonal disease, however, were consistent with toxicity from an unknown substance.

So, I began my own search online for answers as I continued seeking new professional opinion. I read articles from the NEJM and other medical periodicals and began to pick up physicians' language. I joined a blog called Phoenix Rising, a UK-based well-moderated group overseen by a multi-disciplinary gaggle of retired doctors. Research led me to focus on cellular dysmetabolism as my best guess where an answer might lie. After weeks of reading of other men and women who had somewhat related issues, I tried one recommendation—the supplement methylcobalamin.

I took a five-milligram lozenge of the bioactive B12 in the afternoon of the 14th, and the next morning life had changed. I got out of bed, walked into the bathroom, and remarked to my wife, "I have my legs back again." Further, when I increased the dosage of methylcobalamin, I experienced significant cognitive changes that improved my quality of life including almost complete elimination of the brain fog I had experienced for so many years. Terrie tells me I was laughing again—a sound she had not heard for quite some time.

The evidence suggested I had a long-standing, serious B12 deficiency. But that diagnosis was made and treated by the VA years earlier. However, this new discovery explained many historical things including the incidental finding in the late 1970s of the absence of knee and ankle reflexes. It was clear now the deficiency had been ineffectively treated. It appeared, in my case, B12 was in the body in adequate amounts but, inexplicably, could not enter the cells themselves. The standard-of-care maintenance dosage of one milligram of cyanocobalamin daily had not had a discernable effect on the dysfunction at the cellular level. But methylcobalamin in ultra-high amounts was, at least, part of the answer.

I held a clue now about this disease, and over time I learned a great deal more. I pushed the VA for help. I also got an education on physicians and their medical practices. Truth be told, few clinicians are interested in *zebra* cases, the medical slang for those that elude a diagnosis.

The popular saying taught to physicians in med school is "When you hear hoofbeats behind you, don't expect to see a zebra." The meaning of this aphorism is like that of the *Occam's razor* principle, where given two explanations for a set of facts, the simpler is more likely to be correct. Doctors are cautioned they are far more likely to have encountered a horse than a zebra. The lesson—do not get wrapped up in esoterica. The simpler conjecture is likely to lead to the correct diagnosis.

The clinicians I shared my story with numbered into the dozens. Most had no interest in my case beyond the initial office visit. Some, even considering my clinical phenotype, were dismissive enough to suggest my problem was psychosomatic. I would ask, "Okay, that is a diagnosis of sorts but how then do you explain the clinical signs?" That response would usually draw a blank look. They had no idea and wanted me to move along so they could get to the next patient. I have learned to think of the challenge zebra patients face in finding professional help as an unmet clinical need.

But there were Florida physicians whose intellectual curiosity and professionalism emerged, stepping up to meet the challenge. They would take the clinical investigation as far as their charge allowed. To these women and men, I owe a great deal. They include Dr. Tonya Stephenson, neurologist, Venice; Dr. Laura Rainer, endocrinologist, Venice; Dr. John Baga, internist, Venice; Dr. Maida Sierra, psychiatrist, Sarasota; Dr. Kelly Monette, psychologist, Sarasota; and Dr. Sabih Kayan, psychiatrist, Sarasota.

After several years of medical consultations with seemingly whomever would take my meeting, I located a Veterans Affairs geneticist, newly assigned in Las Vegas, who was brought on to stand up a national VA genetics' lab. He was impressed enough with my health summary write-up to call me at home on a Saturday and advise he intended to recommend my referral to a local geneticist. That referral was to a biochemical geneticist at the University of South Florida. She was a pediatric endocrinologist, with a six-month appointment backlog. I was not seen as an urgent case, so six and a half months later, I made my way to the doctor's clinic in Tampa. My presence in the waiting room was a study in contrasts: rows of sick, mostly minority children with young mothers, and me, a white sixty-something male veteran.

Although the Las Vegas doctor had fairly represented my bonafides, smoothing the path for me, over time the geneticist and I did not mesh well. She had ongoing skepticism about my representations, something I was used to seeing from physicians. It took three more years, a formal letter of complaint, and many rounds of disappointment, frustration, and esoteric tests, including one done only by a lab in Zurich, Switzerland, to conclude that she could not help me. She eventually came onboard, though, and told me she had seen many, many rare diseases but nothing like mine. To be fair to her, she was a *pediatric* endocrinologist, and probably not used to weighing the psych profile of an aging male and former combatant.

She recommended I apply for help with the Undiagnosed Diseases Network, a research study group funded by the National Institutes of Health. These were the rare disease doctors, the last stop in America for help in disease identification and potential treatment. As their website informs, it "brings together clinical and research experts from across the United States to solve the most challenging medical mysteries using advanced technologies." The UDN has its coordinating center at Harvard Medical School and twelve clinical sites across the United States. They include Stanford, Duke, Columbia, Baylor, and UCLA. At these prestigious facilities, "doctors and healthcare providers, like neurologists, immunologists, nephrologists, endocrinologists, and geneticists, come together to help find the cause of participant symptoms." I am told the best minds in the medical community are part of the UDN.

I applied to the UDN affiliate at Baylor University in Houston and after an intensive, months-long review process, was accepted for inclusion into the program. The UDN takes on about forty percent of applicants and finds solutions for about nine percent. Euan Ashley, director of Stanford's Clinical Genome Service and its Center for Inherited Cardiovascular Disease, offered about the UDN:

We're learning about biology in a way that could help not just one family, but potentially dozens, even hundreds, of families who suffer that same rare condition. That's the biggest benefit of this network effect — the impact of identifying one patient's disease that could end up being global.

The submission procedure required filling out an online application form, sending all relevant medical records, and two letters of explanation, one from the recommending physician and an optional letter from the patient.

While I was pleased to have my medical case picked up by the Undiagnosed Diseases Network, with the best medical minds in America working on it, I have accepted the progressive nature of my disease. Further, what I have learned through this ten-year diagnostic odyssey is that I have in practice become the model for the advice we give to the men in my combat PTSD group—never give up. While I have no expectation of walking away with a treatment or even a diagnosis from the UDN work-up and consultation, I have learned throughout this process how to mitigate some of the effects of this metabolic disease because I have investigated it and run trials myself. I have not depended on others to find a medical solution. I know that we Viêt Nam combatants, who have much higher than the national average disease rates, must realize that the responsibility for our medical care ultimately rests with us.

The methylcobalamin, alpha lipoic acid, berberine, potassium, and now calcium supplementation have extended my time of mobility and added years to my life by slowing the progressive paralyzing effects of the carbohydrate dysmetabolism. Ten years of my medical research have kept me focused on solutions, rather than idly lamenting the syndrome. I am wearing lower leg braces when I leave the house, and make do by grasping handholds and taking

Looking out my back door

stability from walls as I enjoy my retirement at home. They tell me a walker and possibly a wheelchair are in my future.

My woman has been with me for fifty years, through the tough times when the combat PTSD manifested strongly and made me a suicide risk, and she is still here. In my Southwest Florida home, I enjoy some of the most vivid sunsets imaginable. My friends within my PTSD group are joined with umbilical cords of piano wire, the strongest of bonds, that of brothers in combat.

And when Terrie and I venture beyond our domestic borders, Thor and Lorraine challenge us to pinochle. On regular occasions, Paul Hansen, another Upper Mekong Delta warrior and I shoot games of eight-ball, while taxing each other to remember rock and roll tunes and artists from our youth.

Hey, what more could a guy ask for?

Glossary

1LT	First lieutenant (O-2)
1SG	First sergeant (E-8)
2LT	Second lieutenant (O-1)
75 mm RR	A 75 mm projectile firing weapon with a shaped-charge armor-piercing warhead
ABV	Alcohol by volume
Agent orange	One of many organophosphate defoliants used by the US in Việt Nam
AHC	Assault Helicopter Company
Air America	Airline of the Central Intelligence Agency in Việt Nam
AO	Area of Operations
ARVN	Army of Republic of Việt Nam or army soldier of Republic of Việt Nam
ATC	Armored Troop Carrier modified ACM-6 for riverine combat missions. Also known as Tango boats
ATF	Alcohol, Tobacco, and Firearms
B40/41 RPG	Rocket propelled grenade launcher of type B4 and B41. Widely used by enemy forces to attack fortifications, personnel, vehicles, and helicopters
Baseball grenade	The M76 fragmentation grenade, shaped and thrown like a baseball.

BG	Brigadier general (O-7)
Big Red One	First infantry division of the US Army
C&C	Command and Control
C4	Plastic explosive; a fast-burning charge often used to cut metal such as tresses of bridges
CAR15	Colt automatic rifle-15, a carbine version of the M16
Charlie	American slang for the Việt Cộng
CIB	Combat Infantry Badge
CIDG	Civilian Irregular Defense Group, a US-developed program to advance irregular forces of minority groups in Việt Nam
Claymore	An anti-personnel mine command detonated using an electrical or fused blasting cap
CO	Commanding officer
COL	Colonel (O-6)
COMUSMACV	Commanding general of MACV
CONUS	Continental United States
CORDS	Civil Operations and Revolutionary Development Support
COSVN	Central Office for South Việt Nam; the mobile headquarters of the Việt Cộng
CPT	Captain (O-3)
C.R.I.P.	Combined Reconnaissance (US) and Intelligence (VN) Platoon
Cutout	A mutually trusted intermediary
DIA	Defense Intelligence Agency
DIOCC	District Intelligence and Operations Coordinating Center, the Phoenix office
DITU	Data Intercept and Technology Unit at the FBI
DMZ	Demilitarized Zone

DSLR	Digital single lens reflex (camera)
Extraction	Removal of troops from an area by helicopter.
Fishhook	A geographic peninsula of Cambodia that juts into Việt Nam in III Corps
FNG	Fucking New Guy
GAF	Global Assessment of Functioning score
GEN	General (O-10)
GVN	Government of South Việt Nam
Hooch	A dwelling, sometimes thatched
Horn	Jargon for a military radio or radio handset
Hot LZ	Hot Landing Zone, or area targeted as a helicopter landing zone where enemy resistance was expected
Huey	UH-1H helicopter, also called a slick
IITRI	Illinois Institute of Technology Research Institute
Insertion	Placement of (usually attacking) troops into an area by helicopter
Intel	Elite Vietnamese Phoenix Program squad operating out of Tân Trụ district
ISP	Internet service provider
K54	A prized pistol carried by VCI cadre known as Black Star
KIA	Killed in action
Klick	1,000 meters
Loach	Light Observation Helicopter, the Hughes OH-6 Cayuse
LTC	Lieutenant colonel (O-5)
LTG	Lieutenant general (O-9)
M127A1	White star parachute signal flare

M14	Semiautomatic battle rifle replaced by the M16 beginning in 1967
M16	AR-15 automatic rifle used extensively in Việt Nam by US troops
M60	Crew-served belt-fed light machine gun in wide use by US and VN troops; it fired standard 7.62 mm ammunition at about 600 rounds per minute; the ammunition is the same as used in the M14 rifle
M79	US single-shot grenade launcher with a range of 400 meters; also called a bloop gun
MACV	Military Assistance Command Việt Nam
MAJ	Major (O-4)
MAT	Mobile Advisory Team
Max Ord	Maximum ordinate of fired artillery; the highest point in a projectile trajectory.
MG	Major general (O-8)
MI	Military Intelligence
MSG	Master sergeant (E-8)
NIC	Network interface card
Noncom	Noncommissioned officer
NVA	North Vietnamese Army, or NVA regular; an enemy soldier from North Việt Nam
OCS	Officer Candidate School
OER	Officer Efficiency Report
OJT	On-the-job training
Parrot's Beak	A peninsula of Cambodia in the Ba Tu area that juts into South Việt Nam northwest of Long An province
PCF	Pentagon Counterintelligence Force

PF	Vietnamese Popular Force
Phụng Hoàng	Vietnamese counterinsurgency program known as Phoenix, initially established by the CIA
Porter	Pilatus PC-6 Porter aircraft
PRC-25	The twenty-pound tactical radio widely used in Việt Nam; referred to by GIs as "Prick 25"
PRU	Provincial Reconnaissance Unit
PSP	Pierced steel plank
PTSD	Post-traumatic stress disorder
Push	Jargon for an FM radio frequency
PX	Post Exchange, the soldier's Walmart
PZ	Helicopter Pickup Zone
R&R	Rest and Recuperation
RD Cadre	Rural Development Cadre
Recon	Reconnaissance platoon members of the 2/60 3/9 Army division
REFRAD	Release from active duty
RF	Vietnamese Regional Force
ROTC	Reserve Officers Training Corps
RR	Recoilless rifle
RTO	Radio and telephone operator
RVN	Republic of Vietnam
Sappers	Specially trained Việt Cộng or NVA soldiers who stealthily crawled through barbed wire and other perimeter defenses of a compound with the intent of attacking
Satchel charge	An explosive package hand carried in a satchel or messenger bag with a command detonating device attached

SCG	Static Census Grievance; teams of three to five villagers who collected social and political information from local people in every hamlet to address social injustice and provide a way to win the hearts and minds of the populace
SF	Special Forces
SFC	Sergeant first class (E-7)
SGM	Sergeant major (E-9)
SOP	Standard operating procedure
SP4/SP5/SP6	Specialists in military occupations (E-4/5/6)
SSG	Staff sergeant (E-6)
STRAC	An unofficial 1968 Officer Candidate School acronym for elite troops: skilled, tough, ready, around the clock
TDY	Temporary duty
TNT	Slow-burning heaving charge explosive
TOC	Tactical Operations Center
VCI	The Việt Cộng Infrastructure, or a member thereof
VN	Việt Nam or Vietnamese
VR	Visual reconnaissance, usually by helicopter
WIA	Wounded in action
WOFT	Warrant officer flight training

www.ingramcontent.com/pod-product-compliance
Lightning Source LLC
Chambersburg PA
CBHW040619070526
44654CB00057B/1766